# Raising Kids
# That Succeed

How to Help Your Kids Overcome
Life's Limitations and Think Their
Way to Lifelong Success

"Dr. Lynn Wicker's new book provides a smart, useful framework that allows parents to ensure they're equipping their kids with the tools and beliefs to succeed in the future."

–**Dorie Clark**, Author, *Stand Out* and *Reinventing You*, and adjunct professor of business administration, Duke University's Fuqua School of Business

"Having raised five successful kids myself (total age 203!), I feel qualified to whole heartedly recommend *Raising Kids That Succeed*. Lynn Wicker delivers her wisdom with a compelling and chatty style that refreshes as it inspires. Leave a copy lying around the house and you might just find your kids sneaking a peak at it from time to time."

–**Nicholas Boothman**, Author, *How to Make People Like You in 90 Seconds or Less*

"*Raising Kids that Succeed* changes the game for parents and leaders everywhere – teaching that true influence comes not in ruling with an iron fist, but in leading by example."

–**Cliff Ravenscraft**, Highly acclaimed Podcast Producer of Podcast Answer Man

"Lynn Wicker is first and foremost an educator. She writes information, not from an ivory tower in her office, but from personal classroom experience. If you are looking for a way to give any child an edge in the world of education – this is it!"

–**Dr. Robert Rohm**, Ph.D., President, Personality Insights Inc., Atlanta, GA

"In her book *Raising Kids That Succeed* Lynn Wicker breaks the mold and changes the game of parenting, by putting a new spin on what it truly means to be a leader."

—**Paul Martinelli**, International Speaker and Trainer

"Let me be the first to congratulate you on this 21st Century book. As a published author myself, I know the heart, life, thought and labor that has gone into communicating this message to an audience and generation that desperately needs to change the way they think—especially when it comes to parenting. Not only do I endorse this life changing book, but more importantly I endorse this amazing author! I was attending a major international leadership event in Orlando, FL, with over 1000 leaders in attendance from all over the world. From this crowd is where I met Dr. Lynn and instantly we began to engage in a conversation of great value, as if we had been friends for many years. Just like Dr. Lynn stood out in the crowd with her class, intelligence and purpose, it is my prayer that this book will have the same affect in your life, family and children. If you are ready for your thinking, limits, beliefs and generational dysfunctions to be challenged and changed, then read this book with your children and grandchildren. Blessings and Much Success!"

—**Dr. Craig A. Ponder Sr.**, Ph.D., CEA, CFWC, CFE
Financial Educator, Retirement Expert, Author,
Lecturer and Chancellor

"I love how Lynn really captures what is at the core of successful parenting. She clearly illustrates the power of one's beliefs and thinking, and how they impact our parenting. As a new mom with another one on the way, I feel empowered and equipped to be an even better parent, thanks to Lynn's book *Raising Kids That Succeed*."

—**Melissa West**, CEO of Xtreme Results Coaching

"Lynn Wicker's wealth of experience as an educator and success coach come together in *Raising Kids That Succeed* to help us become the kind of parents our kids need. If you're a student of personal development, you'll discover how to pass on what you've learned to your children. And if you're frustrated or uncertain about whether you have what it takes to be a good parent, you'll find ample reassurance and helpful guidance in these pages."

–**Erin K. Casey**, Author, *Get Personal* and Contributing Editor for SUCCESS Media

"The mindset of success is just that; it starts with your mind. Having a mindset to raise successful children starts with the mindset of the parents. Dr. Lynn has hit a bull's-eye with her latest work on helping parents raise successful children, through practical and usable examples of how to create the proper mindset for both parent and child."

–**Anthony Witt**, Founder of The Champion Entrepreneur

"An unconventional book offering practical, workable advice for all of the ambitious mothers out there, *Raising Kids That Succeed* is an absolute must-read!"

–**Esther Spina**, Best-Selling Author, *The Ambitious Woman* and *The Everything Guide to Network Marketing*

"Nobody hands you a manual when you become a parent. Most of us end up doing the best we can, and often that means we're making it up as we go. Dr. Lynn Wicker draws from her decades of experience, both as a parent and an educator, to offer a roadmap full of practical wisdom. What might happen if we stopped blaming our kids for all the conflict, and looked at our own hearts as parents? What difference might it make if we took the time to know ourselves and our kids as people and connect on a heart level? This book reminds parents to slow down, think intentionally, and plan in advance how we want to interact with our kids. And that's a game-changer."

–**Dave Kirby**, Host of the 1 Simple Thing Podcast

"*Raising Kids That Succeed* is a great book for bettering parents and children alike, and for strengthening the family unit as a whole."

–**Kimanzi Constable**, Publishers Weekly Best-Selling Author, *Are You Living or Existing? 9 Steps to Change Your Life*

"Finally a book that teaches parents how to stop overreacting, and to stop blaming their children! *Raising Kids That Succeed* provides an introspective take on parenting, and emphasizes self-improvement in order to see child-improvement."

–**Lisa Lynn**, Author of *The Metabolism Solution* and Fitness & Nutrition Expert

"What I like about Lynn is that her leadership advice is always very thoughtful, practical and straightforward. This comes from her 30 years of hands-on experience, coupled with great teaching, and her thirst for knowledge. Lynn can always be counted on to come up with the right solution for any situation."

–**Gordon Tredgold**, CEO & Founder of Leadership Principles LLC

"After meeting Lynn at a writer's course in Las Vegas, I knew she was a special person, and was intrigued to see if she was also a special writer. Having now read *Raising Kids That Succeed* I know that Lynn is not only a special writer, but her book also has a special message that will empower both parents and kids. We will be proud to sell it here in the UK."

–**Barry Phillips**, Owner of Knowledge is King

# Raising Kids
# That Succeed

How to Help Your Kids Overcome
Life's Limitations and Think Their
Way to Lifelong Success

## DR. LYNN A. WICKER

NEXT CENTURY
PUBLISHING

**Raising Kids That Succeed**
*How to Help Your Kids Overcome Life's Limitations and Think Their Way to Lifelong Successes*

Published by Next Century Publishing
Las Vegas, Nevada
www.NextCenturyPublishing.com

ISBN: 978-1-68102-087-7
Library of Congress Control Number: 2015949029

Printed in the United States of America

# DEDICATION

*Raising Kids That Succeed* is dedicated to parents all over the world who started their journey as a parent with many hopes and dreams for their kids, only to find that they had more questions than answers in trying to be a successful parent. There's hope! This book is dedicated to parents everywhere who want to learn valuable answers to some of life's most challenging parenting questions. This book is also dedicated to my three children, Weston, Adam, and Lindsay, for all that they taught me about how to be a better person. I love you all!

# CONTENTS

# Raising Kids
# That Succeed

How to Help Your Kids Overcome
Life's Limitations and Think Their
Way to Lifelong Success

# ACKNOWLEDGMENTS

I would like to acknowledge all of the students and their families who I have had the privilege of serving over the past thirty years in public education. My life has been richly blessed by having known you all, and I have learned more than I have taught.

I would also like to acknowledge my mentors, those in my inner circle, and especially author Wayne Dyer, my mentor from afar, for teaching me so much about letting go of excuses, setting my intentions, and allowing me to "see clearly now" how all the events of my life have led me to where I am today. For that I am forever grateful.

# INTRODUCTION

So why read another book about parenting? You may be asking that question as you think back to other books you've read, and the theories and philosophies they had to offer parents. There have been many parenting research studies conducted, written about, and presented to help understand the role and impact of parents in the lives of their children. Through these studies, books, and articles, the authors and experts interpreted their findings, complete with their own insights and opinions, and presented their views. However, the heart and meaning of the information remains about the same. Parents who have read many of these studies and books seem to be seeking the Holy Grail of parenting. When the results they were hoping for with their children don't materialize, there is often frustration and a sense of hopelessness that comes with what appears to be inadequate parenting at best, and failed parenting at worst.

It would seem that with all the parenting resources now available in abundance, particularly through online sources, we would be seeing a large shift in the outcomes of our children in society as a whole. We might think that we should be seeing an overabundance of children who are happy, healthy, and successful, not only now but throughout their lives.

In author Wayne Dyer's book *I Can See Clearly Now*, he talks about his own parenting journey through the years, which led him to write a book about parenting behaviors specifically pointed toward raising no-limit children to become self-actualized adults. He says, "It seems to me that many parents are pushing their children in the opposite direction of the apex of Maslow's pyramid. So many children are taught to live by the demands of their ego—to win at all costs, to accumulate and own as much stuff as possible, to define their lives on the basis of how they stack up to others, to make as much money as possible, and to put a monetary value on everything they do. The results of these kinds of pressures on children show up in personality disorders, obesity, physical illness, anxiety and stress, and emotional instability."

Dr. Dyer goes on to say that in his own research, he asked thousands of parents, "What do you really want for your children?" In his book *What Do You Really Want for Your Children?* He writes that he was fascinated by the responses. He says, "No one says, 'I want my children to be wealthy, to be better than anyone else, to win at everything they do, to get a good job, to get the best grades, to get into the right schools, to look good to their peers.' Yet, this seems to be how they're raising their children."

In her article "The Year of the Awakened Parent," Denny Hagel poses some intriguing questions about the current trends in our society regarding our children and youth. She says, "Parents have to ask themselves the following questions":

- Why in the last year have 84 percent of public schools reported incidents of crime to the police?

- Why has teen suicide had its highest increase in fifteen years? Why then are anti-depressants prescribed for more than 52 percent of our children and teenagers?

- Why has illegal drug use become an unbeatable war, with over one-third of children in the United States using them?

- Why has "bullying" become the number-one topic on the minds of millions of parents?

Despite the thousands of volumes on parenting available, what I now understand is that there has been a quiet shift in the thinking of parents. There is a new sense of urgency and attitude that says, "I don't want my child to become a statistic, so how can I improve?" and "I don't know what else to do, so what am I missing?"

The truth is, even though today's children are growing up in a world that is far different from the world their parents grew up in, there are definitely answers to all the puzzling questions parents face every day. Hagel says that in raising their children, parents are facing challenges for which they have no frame of reference. The parenting skills their parents used seem out of touch and for the most part ineffective. Hagel goes on to say, "Parents really don't need to read the statistics that reflect the increase in drug use, the rise in crime in our school systems, or the rate of increase in drugs being prescribed to children for depression to know about the devastation they see first-hand through their children or through friends of their children." And she's exactly right.

This book's purpose is to provide a new lens through which to see yourself as a parent, but more importantly, to see yourself *first* as a person. This book focuses on who we are as individuals, first and foremost, before we get to what kind of impact we can hope to have on our children as a parent.

I hope to take you to perhaps some uncharted territory in these pages and ask that you simply open your mind and heart, stop looking for "fixes to your kids," and begin to come to an awareness of your own thinking and beliefs that will not only improve your own life and relationships, but will immediately begin to improve your influence and impact with your children. Remember, you cannot give what you do not have.

Let's get started!

# CHAPTER 1

## GREAT PARENTING REQUIRES GREAT THINKING

Sounds like a no-brainer, right? Right. Anyone who's ever been a parent, including me, knows that it's one of the most challenging, even terrifying, jobs a person can ever take on. Yes, I went there; I used the word *job*. Not a particularly invigorating or inspirational word, is it? Instead, the word conjures up all sorts of other words that may include *drudgery, responsibility, thankless toiling,* and *labor.*

There's no doubt that being a parent is a full-time job. But the good news is that mixed in with all of those challenges are also joy, excitement, anticipation, hope, and great feelings of fulfillment. The anticipation of planning for a child, giving birth, and beginning the parent journey is one of the most exciting experiences in life. Seeing a newborn baby's smiles and blissfulness rates right at the top when it comes to feelings of contentment and genuine happiness.

And then it happens…

Somewhere along the way, we realize that we have more questions than answers. We wonder what happened to all the endless bliss and exhilaration, because parenting has taken on a very different feeling. Becoming overwhelmed, afraid, anxious, and even confused is common for all parents sooner or later. For some, those feelings start early, while for others, they might not show up until it's time for those cuddly cheeks to leave the comforts of home to start their formal education. For some, the "Who kidnapped my sweet, innocent child and replaced him with an alien life form?" question doesn't show up until puberty hits. But trust me; sooner or later those feelings will come.

Have you ever wondered why it seems that some parents have all the answers? Why it looks like their kids are always clean, well behaved, and on their way to perfection? Well, don't be fooled. It may appear that way, but I can assure you no parent gets out alive without experiencing the questioning, doubts, and fears that accompany a role that's so high-stakes and important to each of us. I've heard it said that having a child is like watching your heart walking around outside of your body. It's so true.

As parents, we try in vain to control all the environments, circumstances, people, and experiences that might somehow injure or have a negative impact on our offspring. After all, that's our heart walking around out there exposed to the elements! What hurts them hurts us. What wounds them wounds us. And yet we somehow realize how futile it is to completely insulate our kids from what life holds for them—the good, the bad, and the ugly. That is where the frustration and anxiety begin.

In her book *Grooming the Next Generation for Success*, Dani Johnson discusses the need for us as parents to give a great deal of thought to what we are doing to groom our kids for their successful futures. She says, "What I've found in the marketplace, though, is that most successful people aren't really thinking about grooming their next generation. This, I believe, has caused our nation as a whole to suffer in a few different areas. Instead of grooming our kids for success, we are grooming them for absolute mediocrity, and a generation of apathetic kids without drive, dreams, or direction is being raised. And if these unfortunate kids have parents who've sacrificed them on the altar of their own personal success, then these children also have entitlement issues, which is an attitude of expecting something for nothing. How sad is that?"

Dani's point is well taken. It may be a hard pill to swallow, but we have to come to terms with the fact that the same thinking that got us into a mess is not the same thinking that is going to get us out. We have to take a different approach to raising our kids, and it begins with the person in the mirror.

She goes on to say, "It only takes a few good people to step up and start doing something. Start in your home with your next generation. Groom them for success. Many are fooled into believing that they are helpless, powerless, and without the right connections to make a difference. But doing nothing is not going to fix it...Who wants to raise average, mediocre citizens who accept the status quo when the sky is actually the limit? If you don't get them off the wrong path now, you may be intentionally setting them up for a very unsuccessful future." I couldn't agree more with these insights.

We may even find ourselves lying awake at night staring into nothingness and wondering, *Am I a good parent? What in the world is good parenting anyway?* I've given that question a great deal of thought. I've been a public school educator and administrator for almost thirty years, and I've spoken with literally hundreds of parents. I've watched carefully as they've interacted with their kids. And I've learned so much through witnessing their ups and downs, failures and successes. I've also had my own parenting experiences, some of which were my most triumphant celebrations while others, my greatest regrets. From all of those experiences, I've come to understand some important things about the answer to the question, "What is good parenting?"

## What is Good Parenting?

Let's start with just the basics. Most would agree it's pretty obvious that good parenting means providing the necessities of life—the resources your child needs to survive, like food, shelter, and clothing. I also believe good parenting means taking an active role in children's lives from the very beginning, learning everything you can about who they are as an individual, their personality, their interests, and what they are thinking. Building a close and meaningful relationship with your child is just as important to his or her success as the food and shelter you are providing. Trust me on that. It may seem as though believing you are doing an adequate, or even much greater than adequate, job of providing the essentials in life means you're doing enough. But it's pretty clear that without building a solid, ongoing relationship with your child, you are already setting yourself up for trouble ahead.

When we hear the expressions "good parent" or "good parenting," we need to remember they may not mean exactly the same thing as being an effective parent. I've come to understand that being an effective parent means you are taking intentional actions and have intentional behaviors that move you toward the outcomes and successes you want your child to experience now and later in life.

But wait a minute! Intentional actions? Intentional behaviors? That sounds like a lot of work! It also sounds like, as a parent, I'm going to have to do some intentional thinking about all of this.

And there you have it. Great and effective parenting requires thinking. Okay, I've said it. Maybe it's not exactly the news you were expecting or wanted to hear, but it is true. Don't put this book down just yet! I'm reminded of Thomas Edison, who said,

"Five percent of the people think; ten percent of the people think they think; and the other eighty-five percent would rather die than think." Chuckle if you want, but you can't deny that painful truth.

We all want great results, but when it comes down to what we have to do up front to get those results, we tend to revert to the autopilot behaviors that don't really require us to be intentional about our thinking as a parent. We are reminded of this by pastor and teacher Joel Osteen in his book *Your Best Life Now*: "We are set in our ways, bound by our perspectives and stuck in our thinking." How true. But don't give up just yet. Help is on the way!

## Is There an Owner's Manual for Parenting?

When a parenting crisis hits, a long-time often-repeated phrase may be used to supposedly help parents feel better. It simply says that "kids don't come with an owner's manual." That comment sort of lets us off the hook when things start spiraling out of control. It gives us permission to believe there's really not much we can do to increase our influence and effectiveness and actually become intentional in our dealings with our kids. It says, "Hold on, it's going to be a bumpy ride and there's nothing you can do about it!"

But what if there really were an owner's manual to guide our thinking as parents? What if we could all learn to do the kinds of thinking necessary to actually become an effective parent who raises successful kids with their own successful thinking? What if we knew which thoughts actually work for us and which thoughts work against us?

If you are a parent blessed with more than one child, you also know how very different children can be from each other.

And you most certainly also know how different they can be from us! A friend of mine who has three kids a few years apart was talking to me one day about his kids. He said, "I absolutely love spending time with my three kids. Well, maybe except for the middle one!" Ouch. Although he was trying to be funny, I suspect that comment had a great deal of truth in it. We love our kids, but sometimes one (or even more!) just rubs us the wrong way and we can't help but have a greater understanding of why some animals eat their young.

All kidding aside, here's something you don't want to miss: there really is an owner's manual for parents and how we need to think. But how that manual works is much more about us as parents and who we are and our thinking than it is about who our kids are. So the manual works on us and changes our thinking, not theirs. At least in the beginning.

## What Attitudes Do Effective Parents Have?

Attitudes. We all have them. For better or for worse, they set us up for success or utter failure. I absolutely love the quote from Abraham Lincoln, "We can complain because rose bushes have thorns, or rejoice because thorn bushes have roses." Attitudes are what make people see the cloud or the silver lining, the storm or the rainbow, the problem or the opportunity it brings. As parents, our attitudes about ourselves, our kids, and our ability to think differently about being an effective parent are the secret ingredients in our success.

After learning that we have to find a way to engage in intentional thinking about our parenting, we also need to consider which attitudes are necessary to keep the train moving down the track. Effective parents keep front and center an attitude of discovery and learning. They know and understand that they haven't arrived yet with all the answers, but their positive attitude toward personal growth makes them smarter today than they were yesterday, and they are certain that tomorrow they will be smarter than they are today.

Effective parents have an attitude of optimism about their own ability to parent. They learn from their mistakes and focus on the learning, not the mistake. They have an attitude of gratitude. They are grateful for the opportunity to mold and shape a young life, and they are just thankful each day for the responsibility.

I think the importance of having the right attitude in life, and specifically as a parent, is best summed up in this little poem by Walter D. Wintle:

> If you think you are beaten, you are;
>
> If you think you dare not, you don't.
>
> If you'd like to win, but think you can't
>
> It's almost a cinch you won't.
>
> If you think you'll lose, you've lost,
>
> For out in the world we find
>
> Success being with a fellow's will;
>
> It's all in the state of mind.
>
> If you think you're outclassed, you are:
>
> You've got to think high to rise.
>
> You've got to be sure of yourself before

You can ever win a prize.

Life's battles don't always go

To the stronger or faster man,

But soon or later the man who wins

Is the one who thinks he can.

Holding on to the right attitude, despite our circumstances, is one of the very first commitments that we have to make in our thinking if we are serious about this journey in parenting. It's the secret sauce.

## What About Our Beliefs?

We now know that our attitudes are critically important to effective parenting, but before we can go much farther in our "thinking about thinking" conversation, we need to understand that it is just as important to consider our beliefs. What I mean by considering our beliefs is: What is it that we believe about ourselves? What do we believe about our abilities and capabilities? What do we believe about our potential, and, most importantly, what do we believe about our ability to positively impact the lives of our kids and chart a course for their successful future?

Tony Robbins, an American life coach, self-help author, and motivational speaker, defines belief this way: "It's a feeling of certainty about what something means. The challenge is that most of our beliefs are generalizations about our past, based on our interpretations of painful and pleasurable experiences."

So with that definition in mind, if a belief is a feeling of certainty, then effective parents need to believe first in their ability to be an effective parent. They need to have a feeling of certainly about it. Although all of us at times experience self-doubt, it shouldn't define us, nor should we have a "doubt habit" in our thinking as a parent. Being empowered by the belief that you can be a successful parent is critical to being a successful parent.

No parenting book ever written will be of much use to you if you don't first decide to believe in yourself and your own ability to grow and change your way of thinking, when necessary.

We also need to believe that no matter where we are in our parenting journey, it's never too late to learn new ways of thinking and behaving. Some of you may be new parents, while others may have teenagers or even children who are now adults. Some may not even be parents yet but hope to someday give it a whirl. My point is that it really doesn't matter. The only difference in these parents or prospective parents is the age of their children. Your child's age has nothing to do with your ability to make a decision today to change the way you think in your role as a parent and then begin to act on those thoughts. Remember, the owner's manual is all about us, not about the kids. It's never too late to start.

Leadership guru, author, and my mentor, John C. Maxwell, says in his book *How Successful People Think*, "It's hard to overstate the value of changing your thinking. Good thinking can do many things for you: generate revenue, solve problems, and create opportunities. It can take you to a whole new level—personally and professionally. It really can change your life."

I like that statement a lot. It gives us hope that we don't have to remain stuck, frustrated, and afraid. We can actually make a decision to change the way we think and have positive outcomes. That kind of thinking also changes what we believe about ourselves.

## The Power of Reflective Thinking

Most of us have never taken the time to really sit down and do some focused thinking about our beliefs on being a parent. With our busy schedules, we hardly have the time to sit down and think about whether we'll have grilled cheese sandwiches or hot dogs for dinner! But as hard as it may be, it's critically important that we schedule in a few minutes each day to do some reflective thinking and try to learn from that reflection. As John Maxwell says, "Experience is not the best teacher; evaluated experience is the best teacher. Reflective thinking is needed to turn experience into insight."

So a part of our great thinking definitely must include reflective thinking. This tends to be where so many of us fall in the ditch. We have had lots of experiences, both as parents and as kids. When we were children on the receiving end of our own parents' attitudes, beliefs, and thinking, we *definitely* had experiences, right? Later on in this book, we'll talk more about this important piece of reflective thinking on our own upbringing and the powerful influence it had on each of us.

So if reflective thinking causes us to gain insights, then we need to decide today to become more reflective thinkers as parents. There are a few areas that I believe are a great place to begin in reflective thinking as a parent. Let's go!

## How Did You Prepare to Be a Parent?

That may seem like an odd question to you. But in my interactions with hundreds of parents, I have seen the answer vary from "I've read a long list of parenting books and articles," all the way to "Prepare? What do you mean, how did I prepare?" Yep, that's actually the answer I received when I asked one parent that question.

Obviously, it doesn't take a child psychologist to realize that the way people prepare to be parents varies tremendously. Some people prepare to be parents by reading parenting books; they begin to watch others and how they parent, and they may even talk to their own parents in anticipation of having a child. But many people who are about to have children really do not give much thought to how to prepare to be a parent. There's very little thought given to the incredible number of changes ahead and the preparation that needs to happen. Many parents are totally shocked that their child is going to go through so many stages, with unique needs and challenges in every stage. They find themselves totally unprepared, and their lack of preparation leaves them frustrated and desperate. Here are some examples drawn from years of my conversations with parents in various stages of parenting. I've spared no expense in sharing with you some real rib-ticklers. Here goes…

*There's preparation for what you need to know and be able to do during the infant stage.*

Parents should think about: Just how many days can I actually go without sleep and still keep my job? Will my social reputation be irreversibly harmed if I continually show up to work with stinky dried infant formula on my shoulder? Why is it that a grown man can't change a dirty diaper without retching? And finally, is it morally wrong to tell the officer that you were speeding because it was a life-and-death emergency? (Of course, you know the reason you were speeding was because it was midnight and you were on your way to Walmart to buy a new pacifier because the baby woke up again and you couldn't find the old one.)

*There's preparation for and knowledge that is needed for how to be the parent of a toddler who is learning to walk and talk and beginning to do small things for himself or herself.*

Parents should think about: Do I move everything off the coffee table so he can't reach it, or continue slapping his hand while shouting, "No, don't touch," to no avail? Is finding part of a cockroach in your toddler's mouth sufficient reason for an ER visit? Do you have to tell your in-laws the truth when they ask you why the toddler's new favorite phrase is "damn it"? And finally, is there any scientific evidence that an English pea lodged up the nose is really harmful if not removed? (I can't afford another visit to the ER this month!)

*There is preparation to be a parent during the preschool ages when children are starting to learn more academically related things and how the world works around them. This time period also includes preparation for how to get them ready to begin a more structured formal education process.*

Parents should ask themselves: Will my four-year-old appear odd at Pre-K with her binky in her mouth? How can I help all the other Pre-K parents not feel jealous when I have to reveal to them that my child is obviously the smartest, most advanced child in the class? And finally, if my three-year-old can read all the fast-food restaurant signs in town but still doesn't know his colors, is that a problem?

*There is preparation to be the parent of a child that is elementary-school age. This period of time brings many new challenges with becoming part of an organized system of formal education, as well as the social pressures of friendships and encountering and maneuvering through new and different responsibilities during childhood.*

Parents should ask themselves: Is it really socially unacceptable or frowned upon to present my child's kindergarten teacher with a box of Pampers as a part of his school supplies? How can I help my child's first grade teacher understand that it's normal for a child to smear his peanut butter and jelly sandwich all over both the lunchroom table and his best friend Joey? And finally, what's the best strategy for maintaining your self-esteem when you realize you no longer understand your fifth grader's math homework?

*There is preparation for a parent as their child enters into the preteen/ middle school years. It is during these years that many parents often wonder many things about their children.*

Parents should wonder: Where is my *real* child, and who is this horrible imposter living in my house? Is it unlawful to nail your seventh grader's bedroom door shut while he's inside? If I never have the "sex talk" with my middle schooler, does that mean I don't have to worry about her ever finding out about the birds and the bees? (American humorist Arnold Glasow quipped, "Telling a teenager the facts of life is like giving a fish a bath.") If my eighth-grade daughter calls me the "B" word that rhymes with "witch," what are the current sentencing guidelines I can expect for what is going to happen next? And finally, how many part-time jobs will I need to keep my fifteen-year-old son adequately supplied with Twinkies and milk?

I was fortunate enough to be an assistant principal at the middle school level for eight years. Those years taught me a lot not only about that age group of kids, but also about the variety of reactions of parents of middle schoolers. There were definitely some funny moments. At my school we had around one thousand students in grades six, seven, and eight. We used to say that the definition of a middle school student was that they ran everywhere they went and when they got there, they hit somebody. Actually, that's pretty close to the truth! Part of my assistant principal duties was to administer discipline to the students who received misconduct reports from their teachers.

I'd love to tell you that responsibility was one of my most cherished memories, but it would be a lie. It was a great mystery to me, in the beginning, to see how many parents were caught totally off-guard by their middle schoolers' behavior and, even worse, that they seemed to want no part of being the solution. It didn't take long during the parent phone call or conference to know what they were thinking, or not, as the case may be.

One particular parent reaction occurred, somewhat predictably, when a sixth grader was also the parent's oldest or only child. I could always tell by the conversation. It went something like: "I just don't understand it! Craig was a straight-A student all through elementary school, never got into any kind of trouble, and always did what we asked him to do at home. Now he's failing math and science, he's been written up by three of his teachers for misbehaving in class, and last night he slammed his bedroom door in my face when I asked him if he had finished his homework! I just don't understand it!"

And so it goes…

Does that story sound vaguely familiar to you? If you have a middle schooler, I'll bet it does, or at least some version of it does. And let's not forget the incredible social changes that rear their ugly heads in this age group. There are new friendships to maneuver through and hormones raging out of control, and it all begins to take its toll. One day your daughter's playing with Barbie dolls, and the next day she's experimenting with mascara. One day your son's pushing toy trucks in the dirt, and the next day he's flexing his muscles in front of the bathroom mirror. Suddenly, it's like you don't even recognize your child anymore, on any level. It's at this point that parents often get very frustrated, because all the things they used to do don't seem to be working anymore. I once saw a bumper sticker that said, "Parenting is not for cowards." I couldn't agree more.

Let's look at one last preparation stage…

*There is preparation for a parent as their child enters the teenage and high school years. When children reach this age, their parents are either totally exhausted or totally elated that they actually survived their children's middle school years and lived to tell about it.*

*In either case, the high school years definitely have their own unique challenges that require a new kind of thinking for the parent. At this point, teenagers are beginning to see themselves as competent and approaching adulthood. As a result, they often really begin to challenge the adult norms, both at school and at home. This time period for parents becomes especially challenging if they aren't prepared in their thinking.*

Parents should consider the following: Is it just legally or morally wrong to refuse to add your teenage driver to your car insurance policy, which would require you to donate several body organs? If your tenth-grade son is dating a twelfth-grade girl, should you slap him on the back and say, "Atta boy!" or should you be considering what cute version of "Granny" you want to be called? If your eleventh-grade daughter, Amanda, starts doodling on her notebook "Mrs. Amanda Wilson" and her forty-one-year-old Economics teacher's name is Mr. Wilson, should you be worried? If your twelfth-grade son has his heart set on attending Stanford University, but your college budget can only afford City College, should you take out a second mortgage on the house to make his dream come true? And, finally, if your twelfth-grade daughter announces to you and your spouse that she is "coming out" and her girlfriend attends the same high school, do you throw a fit and disown her, pray it's just a phase, or tell her you've always wanted another daughter?

And so it goes…

We often seem to get through the teenager phase exhausted and feeling that the only thing we have left to look forward to is karma. Columnist Doug Larson says, "Few things are more satisfying than seeing your children have teenagers of their own." And I'll repeat once again, parenting is not for cowards.

## What's Next?

So, we've talked a lot about great parenting and effective parenting and how it all requires thinking. It means thinking about your attitudes and your beliefs and reflecting on your experiences in order to gain valuable insights. It's no secret that many people don't give parenting a second thought, much less a first one. And it's pretty clear that parenting, like most complex tasks in life, achieves much greater success with thoughtful, well-considered preparation. Of course, preparation for parenting is no one-trick pony.

There are many stages and phases of physical, emotional, and mental growth that your child will navigate, and each phase has its own unique challenges. Many, many books have been written on the stages and phases of childhood development. That is not the purpose of this book. Obviously, it's very important to be aware of the developmental stages, so do all you can to educate yourself in those areas. For the purposes of our conversation here, we want to create an awareness of our own role as parents and leaders in our child's personal growth and maturity.

As your awareness of what is required for great and effective parenting is being nurtured and increased, you can become armed and ready to move on to the next important element of successful parenting. Remember, it's not enough to just *know* what you need to do. Great parenting has to be intentional.

# CHAPTER 2

## GREAT PARENTING IS INTENTIONAL

If we did a survey of one thousand parents and asked the question, "Are you intentional in your parenting?" my guess would be that many would respond, "Could you please explain the question?" We don't tend to think about something like parenting being stuffed into the same sentence as the word *intentional*. It seems like you either are or are not a parent, right? Well, for the sake of those anonymous survey respondents who didn't understand the question, let's talk about what it means to say "great parenting is intentional."

The Merriam-Webster dictionary defines intentional as "done on purpose; deliberate." I also looked up some synonyms for *intentional*, and here's what I found: *contemplated, considered, premeditated, designed,* and *calculated*. Those words are a little scary. When I hear the word *premeditated,* it's usually during a cop show when someone is being tried in court for murder. When I hear the word *calculated,* I think about the expression "calculated risk" or something that my tax accountant does. But when we really begin to consider these words in the context of being a parent, I believe we may have a lot to learn.

Let's think through this a bit more...

If we are going to use the aforementioned definition, then that would mean that great parents do some things "on purpose." Effective parents are "deliberate" about what they do. They "contemplate" their actions and behaviors before carrying them out. Great parents are "premeditated" in their selection of words and behaviors, and even in their attitudes and beliefs. Parents that are effective "calculate" the impact of their thinking and acting on their kids, both short and long term.

But, Houston, we have a problem...

When I first proposed that great parents also have to do great thinking, it might have seemed like a lot of work to you. Well, hold on to your seat, because engaging in thinking about parenting here and there is child's play when it comes to being intentional! You must be saying by now, "Are you kidding me? You want me to disengage my autopilot setting for parenting and do everything deliberately and intentionally?" Yes, that's pretty much what I'm saying. But here's the good news. As a parent, the more you practice intentionality in your thinking and behaving, the more automatic the effective thinking and behaving becomes.

So little by little, just like most new things we learn to do, the more we practice, the better we get. And when you are raising kids, life makes sure you get an awful lot of practice. But it's worth it. I can't think of a better area of our lives to invest our time, thinking, and energy into being as effective as possible, than raising our kids for success. But what does this intentionality really look like, day in and day out?

## Making Time to Think

I mentioned earlier that it's not experience alone that is the best teacher, but experience that has been reflected upon or evaluated. We all need to ask ourselves some questions: How much focused thinking do I do about how I'm raising my kids? Do I actually set aside time each week to find a quiet spot (yes, they exist!) and do some reflecting on the previous week, being really honest about the decisions I made and the reactions I had? It may seem a little obvious, but for those of us whose lives are literally run by our calendar or date book, we understand all too well that if it isn't on our calendar, it just doesn't happen. Each date on our calendar and all the scheduled meetings, events, and other responsibilities are a portrait of our lives.

Whether we want to admit it or not, what is on our calendar is what gets done. Have you ever had a friend or colleague end a conversation with the proverbial, "Let's have lunch or coffee one day"? I think we've all been there. It has been my experience that if the response isn't, "Okay, let's put that on our calendars and schedule a time to have lunch," then the lunch never, ever happens. If you show me your calendar or date book, I can tell you a lot about your priorities and what you value. You may want to stop reading for a few minutes and take a look at your smart phone or computer calendar and see if you agree. It's a fact that what gets scheduled gets done, and the things we make sure get done are what we value.

So with that being the case, if we are to be intentional about growing in our thinking as a parent and becoming more reflective, then we actually have to schedule time devoted to accomplishing it every day, week, or month, or it just won't happen. I encourage you right now to make the decision to become intentional about scheduling your thinking time and put it on your calendar, then hit the "recurring event" button to make sure you follow through. Remember, being a great parent requires being intentional about scheduling time to think and reflect.

Thinking and being intentional about what we do can be compared to the adage that "actions speak louder than words." We can think casually about our decisions, challenges, and opportunities, or even go so far as to do what has been suggested here and regularly schedule specific times to think. But if there's no intentional follow-through on that thinking and reflecting, it's kind of like putting gas in your car and leaving it sitting in the garage all the time. The car has the potential energy (gasoline) and mechanical ability to drive down the road and take you places, but if you don't get into the driver's seat, intentionally crank that baby up, and head on down the road, you'll be forever taking the shoe-leather express.

## What Do I Need to Think About?

Congratulations! By making the decision to schedule some quality thinking time, you are taking the first step to greater effectiveness in being a parent. Now that you've finally arrived at your scheduled time and gotten all comfy in your quiet spot, what do you actually need to think about?

A great way to begin is to have some way of recording your thoughts and insights, perhaps in a notebook or a journal or on an electronic tablet. If you decide to use an electronic device to record your thoughts, just make sure you have all your notification settings turned off, or the next thing you know, you will be posting a response on Facebook while you are supposed to be reflecting. Hey, it happens to the best of us!

Once you are ready to get started, a good way to begin is by reflecting on the previous week and jotting down any decisions you had to make in your role as a parent and then considering their outcomes. It may be helpful to categorize those parenting decisions into areas, to help you stay focused. For example, you might list school, home, social/leisure time, etc. Or you may decide to just list the decisions freehand and then see if they naturally fall into categories. With either approach, you will be able to see fairly quickly the nature of the decisions you made and even which type or category of decisions seems to take up most of your time. It's an interesting exercise that can help you focus on key places where some intentionality was necessary but, by looking back, you realize that you acted solely on autopilot.

Once you've listed and categorized those decisions, think about the outcome(s) of each decision. Perhaps there were some immediate outcomes that you expected and which were predictable, and perhaps there were some outcomes that you did not expect but were pleased with. Or there may actually have been some unintentional outcomes or consequences—in other words, not only were you not expecting them, but they also made things worse in the long term.

So now that you've identified the outcomes of some decisions, your questions should be: Are you satisfied with the results you're getting from the parenting decisions that you made? Were there any surprises or unintended outcomes that you didn't see coming? Were the surprises or unintended outcomes positive or negative?

It is only when we become intentional in our thinking and reflections about the decisions we make and the actions we take as parents that we begin to stand even the slightest chance of evaluating the results as effective or ineffective.

There are some decisions we make as parents that cause us, after we reflect on the results, to have the following flash of brilliance: *Note to self...never, ever, under any circumstances, do that again!* It's okay. We've all been there. There's nothing wrong with coming face to face with our mistakes or poor decisions. Ignoring them and continuing to repeat them is where we get in trouble. There's no doubt that some decisions have far greater long-term impact than others. The problem is that without thinking and reflecting, it may be too late once the wheels are set in motion.

## Does It Take Both Parents?

Right about now you may be thinking that this all sounds wonderful, but also be telling yourself, *I have a spouse who is forever making poor decisions about our kids, and I just can't make a difference alone!* It's worth pointing out here that this all works much better if *both* parents are involved in the reflective thinking process. If you happen to be a single parent, or a parent whose spouse is not yet committed to being intentional, then you can have the freedom to reflect in solitude. It gets a little trickier when both parents don't live in the same house but still share the parenting responsibilities. If you have the kind of communication with the other parent that allows for it, you can agree to share with each other your thoughts and evaluated thinking about the outcomes and consequences of your parenting decisions.

There is great wisdom in adults cooperating in this area instead of creating a cycle of confusion and miscommunication to kids on what is valued. Putting your differences aside in the interest of raising happy, successful kids is well worth the effort. In any case, if you find yourself going solo in experiencing this personal growth journey and change in your thinking as a parent, you can rest assured that what you do that is intentional will make a difference.

In my conversations with a large number of parents through the years, many have shared that they are definitely not satisfied with the results they are getting as a parent. But when I questioned them about what they were doing to resolve that dissatisfaction, they admitted that they chose to continue on, day after day, making decisions through trial and error, never really understanding the outcomes or why those outcomes occurred. Kind of reminds me of Albert Einstein's definition of insanity: doing the same thing over and over and expecting a different result. I'll let you make the call on that one.

So it all boils down to whether or not you are getting the results that you want with your kids. If you are, then celebrate! If you aren't, then be willing to spend some time reflecting on what you need to do differently and intentionally in order to change your results. But, more than likely, your answer is that there are some areas where you are having great success and other areas that seem to be epic failures. That is a common response I have heard from parents. They thought they were taking the right action or making the right decision, but the results they got somehow fell short. But take heart—learning to be intentional in those areas where you haven't seen as many positive outcomes as a parent is a huge step toward success!

## Stepping Up to the Line of Intent

It may sound a little confusing, but the message here is that you have to be intentional about being intentional. Got it? Stepping up to the line of intent means that you are taking a stand against putting your life and your parenting on autopilot. It means that you are taking a step toward doing whatever it takes to reset your thinking and even taking an inventory of your attitudes and beliefs to make certain they are not unwittingly sabotaging your parenting efforts. It means facing challenges with an intentional commitment to solutions and engaging in actions that move you closer and closer to the goals and success you want to experience in raising your kids.

I'm sure you've heard the old cliché that the road to hell is paved with good intentions. Well, that's not exactly one of the most positive thoughts we can have, but nonetheless, I think there's a message there. Good intentions are misunderstood. What's wrong with having good intentions? The truth is, good intentions without action don't mean or accomplish anything. The good intentions we have to reach all the goals and successes we want for our children will never happen unless we step up to the line of intent and begin to take action. So a little formula for you math enthusiasts might look something like this:

## Thinking + Reflection + Intentionality + Action = Success

Making it all add up is what we really want, but we would be naive to think there aren't plenty of things that tend to get in the way.

## Barriers to Carrying Out Good Intentions

When we find ourselves in a place where our reflective thinking tells us that, yes, we've had some great intentions for a long time, but for some reason we could just never follow through....what then? What kept you from carrying out those intentions? What kept you from trying a new way of thinking and behaving even though what you were doing wasn't working?

Here are a few oldies but goodies that I've been told by parents:

- There's just not enough time in my day.

- I don't have the money or other resources.

- I lack the parenting knowledge.

- I've tried everything I know already.

- I'm a single parent and my ex-spouse keeps sabotaging me.

- My parents did an okay job with me, so I will just do what they did.

- My new spouse (now the step-parent) and I have different parenting styles, and it might create too much conflict if I make too many changes.

- Things are going pretty well, so why make any changes?

I have a confession to make. At one point in time or another, as a parent, I've thought every one of those thoughts. I know it's hard to admit, but when we are finally willing to be honest with ourselves, even though we really do take our parenting role seriously, we've still allowed our perceived barriers to get in the way. These barriers convinced us that our long list of good intentions was just impossible to fulfill. Somewhere along the way, our beliefs, as subconscious and limiting as they may be, did a bang-up job of keeping us stuck in the same cycle of getting the results we didn't really want. So if we can pretty easily identify what it is that we don't want, maybe it's time to focus on what we *do* want to achieve, which are those things we tend to refer to as "success."

## What Does Success Look Like?

One of my favorite quotes is from beloved American baseball player Yogi Berra, who said, "If you don't know where you are going, you might wind up someplace else." Yogi had a knack for mangling his words and rendering some pretty funny quotes. But the profound thing about most of his sayings is that there's usually a whole lot of truth in them if you look closely enough. When it comes to parenting, or anything else in life, if we don't know where we're going, we are most certainly going to end up someplace else. In this whole idea of being intentional, thinking and reflecting, we have to know "where we're going" if we are ever going to know whether we're getting any closer or perhaps heading in the opposite direction.

## How Do You Define Success?

If you travel often, you know that many of us use our smart phone, GPS, or computer when it's time to search for directions to our destination. You probably have a favorite map program or app that is your go-to place for routing your trip. If you are like me, you have more than once entered your starting location and your final destination, then listened to the pleasant voice on the device giving you turn-by-turn directions, only to find out that the destination you arrived at is not where you intended to go. You have a few choices at that point: 1) You can try re-entering the destination address and listening to the dulcet voice on the device saying, "Recalculating"; 2) You can try a different map app and hope for a better outcome; 3) You can stop and ask for directions; or 4) You can just give up and head back home. After all, you probably weren't meant to have your teeth cleaned at the dentist that day.

Funny as all that may sound, I bet you had to laugh a little (or groan) when you remembered yourself having the exact same experience. But what if instead of the destination being somewhere you really didn't want to go anyway (like the dentist's office), your destination was to a banquet where you were the guest of honor?

The problem with the map program directions was still the same, but your motivation to get there, despite several rounds of "recalculating," would be quite different. I don't know about you, but I'll take driving somewhere to receive an award over a trip to the dentist any day!

Thinking about the destination of success in parenting often works the same way. When we begin to consider how we define success in parenting, we have to start with a clear picture of what the intended destination looks like and just how motivated we are to actually arrive there. In parenting, once the destination has been programmed in, there are sure to be some points of "recalculating" along the way. But it's how we think about those times and what we do about them that determines whether or not we actually reach our intended destination.

Many parents whom I've spoken with over the years tend to define success for their kids in a variety of ways. Some common ways include getting good grades in school, being well behaved, making and having good friendships, or excelling in an extra-curricular activity such as sports, music, or the arts. It's often the tangibles that parents will point to as the outward proof that their kids are experiencing success. Things like sports trophies, honor roll certificates, medals, blue ribbons, and scholarships are often the outward measure parents use to gauge the success levels of their children.

But are these things enough? Awards and recognitions of this kind are certainly the outcome of hard work and a cause for celebration...but is there something else? What can we use to help us define success in ways that run deeper than these outward, tangible awards? It's a little more challenging to dig deeper and begin to focus on other ways parents can define success that are, perhaps, not so easy to see or hang on the wall. But I can assure you, it's worth the effort to go deeper.

I mentioned earlier that I've been a public school educator for thirty years, with twenty of those years as an administrator. I've spent many hours thinking and writing about that great wealth of experience and all that those experiences taught me. I feel very privileged to have known and been able to work with literally hundreds of parents and families. I've seen kids enter kindergarten and come out the other end as high school graduates. I've seen and been a part of all the awards and ceremonies for many years. I've been a part of numerous homecoming ceremonies where kings and queens were crowned. I've handed out trophies, shaken hands, and had my picture taken with hundreds of students of all ages. These are all very exciting times and memories that will last these kids a lifetime, but after all is said and done, after the pictures have faded and the crowns have tarnished, what will be left?

We all probably remember the classmate who was voted Most Likely to Succeed in high school. To make matters worse, his or her picture was splashed all across the pages of the school yearbook. Then comes the twenty-year high school reunion and everyone is wondering if the label stuck. Did Gary really live up to his classmates' expectation for a life of success? The answer to that question will most likely be found in the qualities and thinking that Gary had when he left high school—qualities and thinking that shaped his future life beyond his high school accomplishments, and qualities that his parents were intentional about sowing into his heart and mind. Because, you see, his level of life success had absolutely nothing to do with the popularity he enjoyed in high school. His success was a result of something much deeper and much more intentional.

GREAT PARENTING IS INTENTIONAL

## Important Questions That Must Be Asked

So, as a parent, what are your plans and actions for your kids that will take them beyond their outwardly visible childhood and adolescent successes? What will you do to equip them to successfully handle the challenges that life throws their way? What truths do you have for them, while they are still under your influence, that will last them long after the honor roll ribbons and trophies find their way to the attic? How you answer these questions, my friend, will ultimately determine whether you are giving your child the best chance to find their true fulfillment, happiness, and success throughout their life, or whether they will experience their own confusion and perpetual self-doubt.

It's all about our own thinking, reflecting, and intentionality that in turn will be the model for our kids to emulate. As my mentor John Maxwell says, "People do what people see." That's very true. If we want our kids to have actions that lead to lifelong success, we as parents have to provide plenty of mental images for them through our own actions.

Earlier in this chapter, I made the point that if we use the given definition of *intentional* in our parenting, then that would mean that things should be done "on purpose"; that effective parents are "deliberate" about what they do and that they "contemplate" their actions and behaviors before doing them; and that effective parents "calculate" the impact of their thinking and acting on their kids, both short and long term.

But wait just a minute!

What about all those things we do *unintentionally*? What about all of our autopilot attitudes and beliefs that are causing us to make the decisions we make? Is it possible that every day we are behaving in ways we aren't even aware of? Is it possible that we have some beliefs and attitudes that have been "programmed" into us so long ago that we don't even realize their negative impact on us or those around us? Is it possible that those very same negative and limiting beliefs are lurking around in the shadows, too cowardly to come out into the light of day where we can easily defeat them? What about that inner critical voice we all have that regularly reminds us how ineffective and unworthy we are? You know that voice, the one that speaks to us loud and clear and places lids, locks, and limitations on every hope and dream we've ever had. We all experience that voice, and it's time we took it to task.

## So What Exactly is a Limiting Belief?

Seems like a pretty simple question, I admit. But sometimes some of the simplest concepts are the most profound. I'll use an example I think most of us can easily identify with. I certainly don't consider myself a techno geek, but I will say that having to use a computer and computer networks for many years has made me highly conscious of when things are working correctly and when they are not. I notice instantly when my computer slows down to a crawl or a program takes forever to load. On my smart phone, I may realize that I have fourteen programs all open and trying to run at the same time. My poor processor is sometimes on the verge of a nervous breakdown until I remember to shut down some of the programs that don't need to be open all at once.

I like to think of this concept of limiting beliefs as being much like all the programs that are running in the background on our computers, keeping the programs we are actively using working the way we need them to, until... (You know what I'm talking about.) All of a sudden, your word-processing document starts acting goofy. Your computer slows down to a crawl or, even worse, crashes. A call to the Help Desk brings the tech guy running to do a few diagnostics. After a few minutes, he makes the pronouncement that your computer has a virus or a "buggy program," and he's going to have to shut everything down. You'll be out of commission for a few days while he tries to resolve the problem and get you up and running again.

Ugh. Most of us have actually lived through this exact experience, and the worst part about it is our computer was infected and we didn't even know it. There was a pesky computer virus lurking around our hard drive, attaching itself to our beloved programs and causing them to go completely squirrelly.

When I think about these computer mishaps, I can't help but see an uncanny similarity to what happens with us and our limiting beliefs. We all have our thinking "programs" running every day; we use them extensively to make decisions, be productive, raise our kids, and do our jobs. But what if, just maybe, there were some other things lurking around in our human "computers," running in the background without our even realizing it until…it happens.

We get some unexpected outcomes or results from our thinking or decisions. We repeat some old behaviors that we know don't ever work out right in the end, but seem helpless to "reboot" ourselves and select a new behavior. Our thought processes don't seem to be keeping up with the demands of our lives, and everything appears to be slowing to a crawl. And all the while, we don't even realize that there are thought "hackers" that have throughout our lives gained access to us and negatively influenced how we think and behave, all without our even realizing it.

Well, I can tell you one thing for sure. It's happening to us every day. No, it's not a literal bug or virus or hacker. But it is just as damaging and debilitating to our own success and that of our kids.

It's called limiting beliefs. That's right. It's limiting beliefs we have about ourselves that are running in our subconscious background—thinking that can literally cause us to slow to a crawl, have "buggy thinking," or be rendered totally "shut down." Continuing to use the computer analogy, the really scary part about this is that when you are a parent, your computer is tied into a computer network (your kids), and when your computer (you) gets a virus, other computers on your network (your kids) are highly likely to get infected too.

Pretty powerful stuff, huh? But never fear. I'm going to spend some time taking you through exactly what limiting beliefs are and how we identify them in ourselves. We are also going to look at how we can understand the negative impact of our limiting beliefs on ourselves and our kids, should we choose to do nothing about them. And then, lastly, we'll talk about learning how to be intentional in breaking the cycle of unconsciously passing along our limiting beliefs to our kids. When we become intentional about the kinds of empowering and healthy thoughts and beliefs that we sow into the minds and hearts of our kids, we learn how to allow them to be all they were intended to be and to reach their full potential. That, my friend, is what real success in parenting looks like.

As the famous Swiss psychotherapist Carl Jung so wonderfully stated, "If there is anything that we wish to change in the child, we should first examine it and see whether it is not something that could better be changed in ourselves."

# CHAPTER 3

## IDENTIFYING LIMITING BELIEFS

So far, we've discussed the fact that great parenting requires two very important things: great thinking and being intentional. I think we can agree that life in general will be more fulfilling if we are thinkers and reflectors as well as action focused, so giving our attention to these ideas in the role of being a parent is one of the wisest things we can ever do.

Author Dani Johnson says, "As parents, you are the chief influencers in your children's lives. Even if they appear not to be listening to you, they are. You have to take a stand and do your part, even though many adults are going through inner healing due to the absence or abuse of their past chief influencers, the fact remains, parents are the chief influencers and the lack of parental support has a lingering effect on children, even after they become adults."

In other words, if you don't prepare them for their future, someone else will. And you may not like that outcome.

So, then, where do we begin in this process? I strongly believe that our first step as parents is to take a long, honest look in the mirror and ask ourselves what are our own beliefs that have kept us tangled up in our thinking, perhaps even sabotaging our own personal growth and success. In other words, we have to identify those problem areas in our beliefs that impact us in life in general and limit us in our ability to be an effective parent. It's critical that we recognize that parents are, for their children, the primary source of information and belief systems concerning the world, their view of it, and their perception of themselves.

In her book *Becoming an Awakened Parent*, Denny Hagel says that, in the parent–child relationship, there is a two-step process for parents to begin to identify their limiting beliefs. She says the first and most important step is to examine your beliefs and ideas, both conscious and subconscious, regarding parenting, in order to determine your parenting mind-set. She goes on to say that some of your ideas and beliefs you will recognize immediately, while others will take work to uncover. The goal in this process is to remove those negative and limiting beliefs that are passed on to your children without your even knowing it. Hagel calls it "passed-down parenting" vs. "conscious parenting." I like to refer to it as Autopilot Parenting vs. Intentional Parenting.

Inspirational self-help author Louise Hay puts it this way, "We learn our belief systems as very little children, and then we move through life creating experiences to match our beliefs. Look back in your own life and notice how often you have gone through the same experience."

If I were to make a list of some very common limiting beliefs of adults, some would be pretty obvious and some would not. A few of the more obvious ones are: "I'm not smart enough, good enough, attractive enough, or rich enough to _____." Or "I'm too fat, too skinny, too poor, too uneducated, or too old to _____." Then there are those limiting beliefs that are much more subtle: "This economy is just too tough right now." "A person who doesn't have a college degree won't be as successful." "I was never any good at sports, so, naturally, I can't expect my kids to be." "I was never any good at math, so I don't really expect my daughter to be either." "No one in our family has ever done that before, so it's not likely my child will accomplish that either."

And don't be fooled. Limiting beliefs can be very sneaky and blend in with all that we hold to be true and sacred about life, while all along, they are secretly robbing us of our potential, our dreams, and our ultimate joy and happiness. They are like Trojan horses masquerading as beliefs that serve to keep us safe and secure, when in reality they are stealing us blind without our knowledge.

When we finally do summon the courage to call something out as a limiting belief, the tragic part is that we tend to not even make an effort to challenge it, to test its true limits. We just go right along, believing it, living with it, and ultimately living out its consequences in our daily lives. It often shows up in a way that stops us dead in our tracks, keeping us from stretching out to touch our dreams. We may believe we are too old to go back to college; we may believe that we are not pretty or handsome enough to ask a particular person out on a date; we may believe that we are too old to start a new career; or we may believe, for no apparent reason, that our earning capability has a certain ceiling. All of these limiting beliefs and hundreds more like them are hidden culprits, running in the background, all along sabotaging our success. And since it's our belief system that dictates who we are and who we become as individuals, they most definitely impact how we parent and, ultimately, how successful our kids are in life as a result of our parenting.

Of course, many of the decisions we have made in life, based on limiting beliefs, are fairly inconsequential. For example, I may believe that I'm too old to train for the Olympics, but since I don't have the desire or need to be an Olympic athlete, I'm really not concerned about that one. But the limiting beliefs that get in the way of our dreams and success in life are the ones we must become aware of, test their validity, and put to rest!

So how do we begin to identify the limiting beliefs that are important enough and impactful enough to uncover? The obvious place to begin is to take a hard look at your life and the results you've been getting. The results we get in life are not a mistake. It's what we have produced based on what we believe to be true. It may be a conscious thing or an unconscious thing, but whether we like it or not, we get in life who we are and what we believe to be true. This is certainly true in our parenting experiences.

Begin by taking a good look at the results you've gotten over time and think about those results. Are you pleased with them? Are you frustrated and bewildered at some of the outcomes you've experienced with your kids? These questions and their answers are the beginning steps in this parenting/thinking/intentional journey.

Here's the good news. Once we've taken a long, hard look at our "life results/parenting results," they can be very revealing! And even more good news is that if the results we've gotten are not the results we wanted, it's probably due to some tucked-away limiting belief that's been trouncing around in our subconscious, wreaking havoc with our lives. I don't know about you, but I believe that's a great place to start! It's a wonderful feeling of empowerment to know there is a sort of inventory we can take in our lives to see what is working and what isn't. Once we learn that, we will have some excellent insights into uncovering our limiting beliefs.

What are some common areas where people struggle? Remember, these general "life" struggles are most certainly going to bleed over into your role as a parent and create the same struggles there. So when we are thinking about any and all areas of our lives that could be causing us difficulty due to our limiting beliefs, don't think you can just separate areas of your life into silos and keep things all neat and compartmentalized. Who you are as a person is who you are as a parent. That is very true.

Allison Foskett, author of *How Smart Women Achieve Big Goals: Motivation to Focus and Follow Through with Your Life Dreams*, introduces a goal-setting program that includes seven steps. Step 6 in this program is Identifying and Overcoming Limiting Beliefs. Allison says that "the beliefs that you hold are either empowering, or dis-empowering. It should never be a question of which belief is right versus wrong." She goes on to explain that your mind-set and your ways of thinking either help you or hold you back. I found her list of what limiting beliefs really are very helpful.

Her list for understanding limiting beliefs includes:

- Excuses

- Negative thoughts

- Justifications

- Worries

- Beliefs conditioned from culture or family

- Thought patterns

- Perfectionistic thinking

- Past failures

- Fear

- Any other ways of thinking or cognitions

Allison also provides a list of helpful questions to help identify limiting beliefs. I've added some details in parentheses to help you focus more on the role of parenting, and I've provided a non-parenting-focused general answer as an example to each question to help get you started thinking.

1.  What rules have I created in my life that could be limiting my ability to get started with my goal (in the context of this book, goals with regard to parenting)?

    *e.g., I cannot change—it's in my blood/family.*

2.  What pessimistic thoughts reoccur in my head every time I think about pursuing this dream? (of being a more effective parent)

    *e.g., I'm not good enough to achieve anything.*

3.  What unnecessary assumptions do I make about achieving and committing to this goal? (in improving my parenting)

    *e.g., I'm helpless to change things.*

4.  What limiting clichés, quotes, aphorisms, or other catchy phrases do I entertain in my head? (as I think about what I believe I know about parenting)

    *e.g., What can go wrong, will go wrong.*

5.  What stereotypical beliefs or cultural myths am I allowing to hold me back? (or what about how your own parents parented you)

    *e.g., This is a man's world.*

6.  How might my standards about "what" and "how" things should happen, be negatively affecting my ability to go with the flow and make things happen? (standards I know about parenting)

    *e.g., I've always done it that way.*

7. Are there any values that I'm holding onto that interfere with me achieving this goal? Do I value something that contradicts what I want to move toward? (values that perhaps belonged to your parents?)

   *e.g., I should never rise above how I was raised.*

8. What self-defeating meanings have I created based on my past failures with important goals? How do these meanings limit me and become barriers to goal setting? (past parenting failures)

   *e.g., I will never be successful.*

9. What disempowering stories, narratives, or mental scripts do I play over and over in my head? (that make me feel ineffective and like a failure as a parent)

   *e.g., Why does this always happen to me?*

10. Do I hold onto any black-and-white philosophies that keep me frozen in a passive way? (family norms or history about parenting)

    *e.g., There is only one right way to do something.*

As you think through these great questions, take some time and write out your answers. When you come back to them later on, you may find that your list is not that unique.

As you review your thoughts to the preceding questions, it's helpful to know that there are many areas where people commonly have major challenges in their beliefs. One area commonly listed as an area of personal struggle is finances. Maybe your bank account and income-to-debt ratio is not exactly what you had in mind when you ventured out on your own, got your first "real" job, and settled into life as you now know it. Perhaps you have more debt than you expected you would have, and for some reason, all your attempts to turn that pattern around just aren't getting the desired results. Did you ever think that maybe there are some unrecognized limiting beliefs at work here? Perhaps you've been told you are poor and you may as well accept that and not try to do any better financially. Maybe you believe your middle-class family income is what you are destined to always have because, after all, your parents raised you with a middle-class income and you turned out just fine.

It doesn't matter at which end of the financial spectrum you find your thinking, any limiting thoughts and beliefs you have will completely sabotage you without your even knowing it. Your limiting beliefs will actually prevent you from being aware of an opportunity to radically change your financial situation. Your limiting beliefs about your financial success will keep you stuck right where you've always been.

Guess what? Your kids watch you, listen to you, and learn from you. They learn what they believe to be true about money and finances from what you do and say, and if you've placed limits around yourself with some beliefs that aren't serving you, those beliefs will most certainly be passed right along to them. As you think about that, does it make you feel depressed or elated? It's very important that you are honest with yourself in how you answer the questions listed above, so you can really begin to do some thinking about which thoughts and beliefs are limiting you.

What about your personal beliefs concerning health and investing in your personal well-being? Perhaps you are a person that begins a new diet in January, complete with gym membership, hoping to finally lose that extra weight and "get fit." Maybe this is the fifth year in a row that plan has not produced the results you wanted, and you just can't figure out what keeps derailing you. Sure, you can find plenty of convenient excuses to help ease the pain of unfulfilled goals, but maybe you would do yourself a greater kindness by being willing to explore which beliefs you have lurking just below the surface that ultimately limit you in achieving your goals.

You might find that all the "inner critic" voices are telling you that because you come from a family that's always been overweight, it must be your destiny. Or maybe you had a weight challenge growing up and still hear those voices calling you "chubby" or "husky," and you still carry those labels inside your head, speaking to you with words of condemnation that simply won't allow you to achieve any other body type than the one your belief system limits have placed upon you.

And just like with the money conversation, your kids are watching, listening, and learning from everything you do and say and will easily conclude that your spoken and unspoken beliefs about food, body weight, body image, and living a healthy lifestyle are the correct beliefs for them to adopt. All this teaching and learning goes on much of the time without anyone even being aware that it is going on. And yet the stakes are so very high in this process, as all of this transmission of limitations will guide your kids straight into their future lives.

Is your inventory of "life results/parenting results" loudly telling you that you just aren't producing the planned results in certain areas of your life and in parenting your kids? Are there areas in your life where, year after year, you just can't seem to make the progress you were certain you could make? When you identify these places, it will be the beginning of uncovering the limiting beliefs that persist in yielding the same old results. Just as in police work, making a positive identification of the "suspect" is the first step in the investigation. Once you've started identifying those limiting beliefs you suspect are derailing you and, ultimately, your kids' success, you are well on your way to removing them from holding you back.

Once you believe that you've identified some of your limiting beliefs and have determined that they are so limiting you would never want to unwittingly pass them along to your children, what steps can you take next? Author Dr. Matthew James, president of the Empowerment Partnership, created a very effective four-step process for dealing with limiting beliefs once they've been identified. I think this process is a very practical one that has to be repeated over and over for us to develop a healthy habit of challenging beliefs that are subconsciously sabotaging our own success, as well as our success in being an effective parent.

## The Four-Step Process

Step 1: Write the limiting belief down. Play detective and follow your thoughts and emotions to discover the limiting beliefs that hold you back. Put them on paper! You might note how strong each belief is and what emotions they elicit in you. List those that limit your life generally, and then be more specific and list those that limit you in your role as a parent.

Step 2: Acknowledge that these are beliefs, not truths! This is often the hardest step. "But—but—my limitations are real!" Here's the place where choice comes in. Which are you more interested in, defending your limitations to the death or achieving your goals and desires? As author Evelyn Waugh wrote, "When we argue for our limitations, we get to keep them." You choose.

Step 3: Try on a different belief. Use your imagination and try a belief that is aligned with what you want. It might be something like, "My financial difficulties in the past have taught me so much that I'm fully prepared to handle them now!" Or, "Now that I've experienced what it feels like to be unsuccessful in my weight-loss goals, I'm fully prepared to think differently about my health and begin to make progress!" The trick is to go beyond just saying it. You want to really step into this new belief and find out how it feels. Done thoroughly, Steps 2 and 3 will go a long way toward dismantling your old limiting decision.

Step 4: Take different action. This might feel scary, but act as if your new belief is true. If you really are capable and have learned a tremendous amount from past financial difficulties, what steps would you take now? If you really are the kind of person who eats healthy food, what will you put in your grocery cart? If you are the kind of parent that sets clear boundaries for your kids, what would you say and do? If you avoid taking any steps based on your new belief, you will just feed your old limiting belief. Taking action, even the smallest step, will help solidify your new un-limiting decision. Your first steps don't have to be perfect, just headed in the right direction. And be sure to acknowledge yourself when you've taken that step. Celebrate!

These four steps in the process of dealing with limiting beliefs have to be taken over and over, until the new beliefs you are cultivating have firmly taken root. You will be amazed at how this will happen over time if you are consistent with becoming more aware of how your beliefs have been leading you around by the nose, with or without your conscious mind's permission!

And it's extremely important to remind yourself that it's not enough just to "seek and destroy" limiting beliefs, but as mentioned previously, to create new beliefs as well. Author Allison Foskett also has some helpful questions to help create new beliefs.

1.  What adjectives or words could I use to describe myself that make me feel good?

2.  What evidence do I have that disproves the limiting belief?

3.  What evidence do I have that proves just the exact opposite of this limiting belief?

4.  Look for a list of positive beliefs on the Internet. Do any of these ways of thinking actually resonate with me and make sense on an experiential level? How can I adjust them to be true for me?

5.  How can I turn my limiting belief into a new, idealistic way of thinking?

6.  What is the exact opposite (positive) way of thinking about this limiting thought pattern?

7.  How do other people who hold the opposite belief of mine think? What positive ways of thinking are working for them?

8.  How can I create empowering beliefs by creating my own quotes, aphorisms, or life philosophies that will support my goals?

9.  What is the belief or thought system that I wish I could truly believe? Turn this into a positive affirmation by starting it off with, "I'm in the process of thinking..." or simply adapt a pre-existing affirmation into a belief system that works for you.

10. Think of a person who has already achieved your desired goal. What attitudes, ways of thinking, and mind-sets did they adopt in order to be the successful person they are?

## More Help with Identifying Limiting Beliefs

Author Joel Falconer warns us that it's not only our current limiting beliefs that can affect our behavior and thinking; it's also the beliefs we've held in the past. This includes, of course, those beliefs that we were brought up with as children. What is so interesting is that even when we become adults, if we've totally shifted our perception of reality 180 degrees, the effects and impact of those early childhood beliefs can surface anytime and last for a lifetime. Joel states that, "Limiting beliefs are simply assumptions about reality that are not true. In order for our actions to have the greatest positive effect, we need to have beliefs that are as close to the reality as possible—deceiving ourselves will take us farther from the goal. So, a limiting belief, when it comes down to it, is a belief that isn't true."

You don't need many years of living under your belt to come to the conclusion that at times our perceptions and reality are fundamentally two different things. That being said, we will always have limiting beliefs of some kind. Even though we can agree with that statement and conclude that it is impossible to ever rid ourselves of all limiting beliefs, with some intentionality, exploration, and a willingness to be open to new information, we can begin to eliminate those limiting beliefs that don't work for us and, most importantly, that we definitely don't want to pass along to our children. The goal in this process is to close the gap between reality and what we perceive reality to be.

Joel Falconer, in his blog post "Find and Replace Limiting Beliefs," outlines three important steps in this important process of closing the gap between reality and our perceived reality:

1. Observation

2. Openness to new information

3. Trialing new information, otherwise known as trial and error

1. Observation

> Observe the world to see what works and what
> doesn't work. Just taking a different viewpoint
> when observing can dramatically change how we
> interpret what we are seeing. It's likely that some
> of our limiting beliefs derive from the viewpoint
> that we have always had about a particular event or
> circumstance. Whether we view from an optimism
> or pessimism, a conservative or liberal, or a poverty
> or abundance mentality, the interpretation will be
> very different.

Joel Falconer asks an interesting question: "What is observation? I always assumed that people would automatically know what I mean when I tell them to observe. In personal development, it is necessary to 'observe' without having a specific target in mind. It's a required state of mind to find both new ideas and bad habits. The other day I was talking about this concept of limiting beliefs and observation with a friend who said, 'What do I observe?' and since then it has been obvious to me that it's not an entirely intuitive practice."

Being in the moment and truly becoming a thoughtful observer of our surroundings takes practice. It requires us to be willing to become more aware of what is going on around us and to take intentional note of it instead of living in a more passive mode where we really aren't giving much thought to what is happening right under our noses. Falconer says, "Take note of your surroundings and be aware of them, instead of just existing in them. It's not difficult to teach yourself this, in terms of the skill and knowledge required to do it, but it does take time and discipline before you'll habitually stay in that mindful zone."

When we engage in this type of mindful observation, we are really learning to spot occurrences of disconnects in beliefs, or places where perception doesn't match up with reality. So when we practice this type of observation, we can begin to see many examples of mismatched beliefs/perceptions with reality. Not only can we see it in ourselves, but we can see it happening to the people around us. Let's talk about something specific to parenting. Here's an example of what I mean:

Suppose your child is trying out for the local soccer team. At the tryouts, you notice, through mindful observation, that your child is smaller, slower, and less skilled than the other children on the field. You immediately begin thinking to yourself that there is no way your child is going to make the team, based on your quick observation and comparison of your child to the other participants. You have made a decision, even before the tryouts begin, that this is not going to be a fair process because the majority of the other kids are all on traveling soccer teams and have had much more experience and opportunity to play than your child. Before the tryouts even start, your anxiety level and agitation at this "skewed" process grows higher and higher, and your child senses your nervousness and becomes anxious as well. Your child now has a stomachache and says he doesn't feel like trying out for the team and wants to go home.

## Limiting Belief Rewind and Fast Forward

You remember being around the same age your child is currently, when you tried out for the softball team. Your memory of the experience is a horrible one in that you were much smaller than the other kids and your parents couldn't afford for you to play on a traveling team, so your experience was limited and you never were selected for the team. As a result, your limiting belief or perception of today's experience with your own child was that he would never be picked for the team.

While at today's tryouts, at the moment you began to think about all the reasons your child would probably not be picked for the team, you could have challenged that belief by asking yourself if your image/perception of what was happening was, in fact, reality. You could have required yourself to be patient and let the process work itself all the way through before becoming outwardly anxious and frustrated, having already decided that something terribly unfair was about to happen. With that approach, your child would not have become more anxious due to your increased anxiety and could have completed the tryouts.

When you practice this type of mindful observing, it becomes much easier to spot your perceptions/beliefs that are somewhat distorted from reality, those mismatches that we talked about previously. This gives us an idea of which of our internal beliefs need to change.

As Joel Falconer says, "When you successfully do this for the first time, it's a pretty enlightening moment—like seeing something with absolute clarity for the first time; like taking your sunglasses off and finally seeing all the color and depth of your environment."

And clarity is exactly what we are after. The clarity that comes with being honest with ourselves and confronting our limiting beliefs is one of the most exhilarating experiences we can have in life. We need to get clarity for not only our own benefit, but also for the benefit of our kids as we strive to be better parents.

2. Openness to New Information

An extremely important prerequisite to successfully replacing a limiting belief is having openness to new information. Many people get tripped up at this point because they are so married to their existing beliefs that they can't fathom allowing a new piece of information to begin to erode them. Openness to new information is very important to seeking your own limiting beliefs and replacing them. You will find that if you're open, you'll allow yourself to see a circumstance, event, or action in the way someone else sees them.

Falconer says, "Using the experience and beliefs of others to test your own is a massive shortcut to the process of finding and replacing limiting beliefs. This works best when others have fought their battles hard to find the optimal belief in an area, and you no longer have to because you've been open to their ideas. If you want to quit smoking, read about how other people have successfully removed harmful habits from their life and apply the beliefs that enabled them. The belief that it's impossible to quit is usually the one that keeps people addicted."

It is imperative that you be open to new ideas if you want to replace those limiting beliefs that aren't getting you to the outcomes you really want. The irony is that being open to new ideas is a belief in itself! You can actually be completely sabotaged at this early stage by believing that you are, in fact, not a person open to new ideas. You simply cannot remain in any way close-minded if you are on a journey to eradicating as many limiting beliefs as possible. If you don't change that, there's absolutely no point or benefit in trying to go any farther in this process.

There is an important point to be made here about what being open to new ideas looks like. Most of us would be open to, and even welcome, a new idea as long as we think it is a good idea. That's not the problem! The problem comes when the new idea is one that we either completely disagree with or, at best, just don't like.

Taking a healthy approach when contemplating a new idea that may seem completely foreign is to view it as interesting, worth exploring, and something that piques our curiosity. Taking that approach with ideas that we like *and* with those that make us uncomfortable will help lead us to be more accepting of them. Remember, we must go outside our comfort zones because there is absolutely no growth inside of them.

A final word on the consideration of new ideas is, always remember that I'm not suggesting we blindly accept all new ideas that come our way. On the contrary, we should be as objective as possible and, if the new idea simply doesn't measure up, then we should reject it. As Joel Falconer quips, "Accepting every idea the world throws at you is a practice known as stupidity." That's something I think we can all agree on!

3. Trialing New Information (or Trial & Error)

So at this point, we are mindful observers and we are also being open and exploring the existence of new ideas and being objective about the validity and practicality of those new ideas. Just as with most things in life, we can watch and think, but we'll never really find our own limiting beliefs until we actually try some new ones in their place.

It's kind of like conducting an experiment to see if the outcomes and results that you are getting are improving when you try out a new idea that is replacing an old belief. Trying out some improvements to an existing idea or belief can even make a difference. You need to do this for at least seven to thirty days—the longer the better. Trying the changes or improvements for a few hours or a day or two will not give you enough time to know if there really was a positive change. A short time frame really just tells you that it was uncomfortable to try something you weren't used to doing. It takes time to get over the newness of being uncomfortable, so take that into account.

During the "trial" process with a new way of thinking, you may find that you actually enjoy the change in thinking or doing. You may also find there is a certain exhilaration that comes with adjusting to a new belief and that this becomes a positive source for exploring even further.

Once you have decided upon the length of your trial period, stick with it. When you come to the end of that time, if you have any doubts, you should stop for a few days and go back to your previous thinking or doing and evaluate the difference as objectively as possible. The critically important word here is objective. That objectivity means making sure you are doing all things possible to remove emotions from helping to determine if the new idea, thinking, and action was an improvement. There is no doubt that it is definitely a challenge to remain objective, but just being aware of the need to be objective will help.

I've shared with you some steps and approaches for first becoming aware of your limiting beliefs and provided some questions for you to think about and jot down your answers. It's important to actually write down your responses and keep your notes handy. As you become more aware and engage in mindful observation, you will find yourself continuing to add to your list of the beliefs that are limiting you, in particular in your role as a parent.

By now, I think it's become pretty obvious how high-stakes this thing called parenting really is. As a parent, you literally hold the future of your children's lives in your hands, and your commitment to your own self-discovery, awareness, and behaviors is 100 percent connected to your child's success.

So what are the consequences and impact of failing to commit to this self-discovery and personal growth? What are some of the common pitfalls, anxieties, fears, and worries that parents experience in their parenting journey? The next chapter will explore these impacts and consequences, as well as some comments from parents who shared their worries and fears about raising their children.

# CHAPTER 4

## THE IMPACT OF A PARENT'S LIMITING BELIEFS

As I've stated, limiting beliefs can be a nasty, hidden thief that robs us of our power and ability to realize our full potential in life. Once we begin to experience some success in identifying those limiting beliefs, we are on our way to isolating them and replacing them with beliefs that are affirming and empowering and that ultimately lead us to be more effective in our parenting. There is simply no way we can effectively groom our kids for success when we are constantly on autopilot in how we live and parent. And, as the subtitle of this book states, our goal is to help our kids overcome life's limitations and think their way to lifelong successes.

At this point, you've read enough to have a good understanding about what limiting beliefs can do to us, but sometimes it helps to actually see the sabotaging and debilitating impact of our limiting beliefs, not only on ourselves but also on our kids. Sometimes, that's what we need to be motivated to become serious and get real about the personal work it's going to take to experience personal growth in this area. It's never a completed job; it's a journey that we are all on.

In working with parents for many years, in schools and also through the use of parent interviews, I've discovered that one of the primary areas where limiting beliefs tend to hang out is in our fears and worries. Let's take a deeper dive into what this looks like in some real situations.

## What Parents Had to Say

As I was preparing to write this book, it was critically important for me to learn parents' answers to a few questions that I believed would give a glimpse into the minds and thinking of today's parents. It's one thing to speculate or share my own personal experience about limiting beliefs as a parent, but I wanted to go straight to parents and ask them to respond to some questions about their fears and worries as well as the resources they access to help them in their parenting role.

Why did I ask specifically about fears and worries? Statements of fear and worry often provide important clues to the underlying limiting beliefs that are lurking in our subconscious. Those fears and worries are often symptoms of a faulty belief system that we have as adults and need to challenge.

To help me with this information-gathering process, I created a short online survey for parents. The respondents were a cross-section of parents whose kids were in kindergarten through twelfth grade. The parents represented a wide range of demographics, including varied socio-economic status, racial diversity, and educational attainment levels. Therefore, it's highly probable that these responses are not atypical for the broader group of parents residing in the United States. There were a total of 138 survey respondents.

The survey included five questions, two of which were open ended and three of which were selected response:

1.  What are you most afraid of when it comes to parenting?

2. What do you worry the most about as a parent?

3. How often are you getting the results with your child that you thought you would get?

4. How often do you experience "epic fails" in parenting and you just don't understand why?

5. How often do you read parenting books, magazines, or blogs?

I will take each survey question and share some of the parent responses for questions 1 and 2 about fears and worry. But before you go any farther, here's what I'd like for you to do. Go back to your notebook or journal and answer these five survey questions for yourself right now. It's important that you stop and take the time to do this, because after you've read the other parent responses, I'm going to ask you to do one more thing. It's worth doing! So place a bookmark on this page and take some time to answer the five survey questions listed above. Ready, set, go!

## Parent Survey Responses

If you're reading this section, I'm celebrating with you that you took the time to sit down, do some thinking and reflecting, and jot down your own answers to the five parent survey questions. You'll need to keep your responses handy as you read on.

I'm going to first focus on only the first two questions of the survey, which were the two open-ended questions. I will discuss the results of the last three questions later in this chapter.

After my review of the parent responses for questions 1 and 2, I discovered something very interesting. Out of 138 responses overall, the responses concerning fears and worries seemed to fall into four distinct categories, with only a couple of responses that did not. I organized the responses by these categories and will discuss them in this fashion.

## FOUR CATEGORIES OF PARENT RESPONSES

1. Personal Failures as a Parent

2. Future Success/Happiness of Child

3. Safety and Security of Child

4. Negative Outside Influences on Child

As you read through the parent responses, get out your list of responses. Place a check mark beside items on your list that you also see listed in the parent responses. If you see a survey response that resonates with you as a fear or worry you also have had, feel free to add it to your own list.

For each survey question, I am providing the parent responses according to the four categories. You will also notice I have included the percentage of responses that fell into each particular category. It's interesting to note those percentages and get some sense of which categories were more prevalent for each question. I'll be discussing the significance of those percentages in the next chapter.

I encourage you to take your time as you read through these parent responses. They are simply listed in bulleted format, so you may be tempted to just scan down through them. But I want you to go slowly through the lists, paying attention to your own mental and emotional reactions to them, because those reactions are great cues that perhaps a particular fear or worry listed is one that you've also had, but it was not fully in your awareness until you saw it in print. If you take this activity seriously, there is the potential for some powerful learning about your own limiting beliefs.

In the next chapter, we will be using your list of responses to begin putting the pieces of the puzzle together. And in the final chapter, we'll be taking a look at an important action plan for *Raising Kids That Succeed!*

1a. What are you most afraid of when it comes to parenting? 64 percent said Personal Failures as a Parent.

- Being a bad influence on my kids through my own weaknesses

- Passing on my fears/challenges

- That I'll do something that will damage my child or will damage others

- The unintentional baggage I pass on

- Not being the best example

- Hoping that my mistakes in parenting will not scar my children

- Failing

- Making the wrong choices. I always base my decisions on what I think is right. As you know, hindsight is 20/20.

- That I will disappoint my child or that he will feel unloved

- Failing to be a good example of following God so my kids can see how God uses us, helps us, and listens to our prayers when we are obedient to His will for us

- Failing, and making sure we are raising our children correctly through discipline

- That I am somehow going to "screw something up" and my kids won't reach their potential for success, or that because I push them to be successful, they will resent me

- I am afraid that I am forgetting to teach them something they will need moving forward into their adult life. I am afraid that I am not teaching them or giving them the fundamentals of being Christians, which I truly believe will help them to not make decisions on a whim or due to selfishness.

- I am most afraid that I fail—as a parent—to instill in my children the right balance of love, confidence, attention, exposure, and respect and compassion for others, our community, our world.

- Failing; not being there for them when and how they need me; being the role model and influence they need to be happy and successful

- That I won't be successful at instilling the values they should have

- That I'm not giving my child the best childhood ever

- Not being there enough for my kids

- Losing a connection along the way; losing credibility with my kids

- Dying before they're independent

- When it comes to parenting, I think we are most afraid of failing to provide every opportunity that we can for our kids to succeed in our ever-changing world.

- That a personal shortcoming will adversely affect my child

- I am afraid that sometimes my husband and I have different values on how to raise our children and that with two different parenting styles, we will send mixed messages that may confuse the children.

- Being overprotective and the balance of parenting versus allowing my child the freedom to experience life

- Failing in my marriage and becoming a single parent

- I am scared that I will not be able to answer the difficult questions in life. I want to be able to give answers or provide direction that satisfies their curiosity without giving them unrealistic expectations of life, while not crushing their spirit or curiosity.

- Failing to prepare him for the "not so great" people and things he will encounter in the world

- I am most afraid that I will fail to be the role model they need and exhibit behaviors that I don't want to see in them.

- Making the right decisions

- Not recognizing my child's way of learning/ personality and pushing them to conform to being something they are not

- Making the wrong decision about one thing or another

- I won't say that I am afraid, but I am sure every parent has experienced a time when they questioned their parenting skills and implementation of them.

- That I will not have prepared my child for real life

- Making bad decisions for my child

- That I'm missing important struggles or challenges she may be experiencing because she chooses not to discuss with me or another responsible adult but rather discusses with friends/peers who may give bad advice, or she discusses with no one. I believe we have an open relationship, but sometimes teens may keep things from parents because they feel parents may not understand or it is too "bad" to reveal.

- I found myself fearing failing to raise children that are independent. Will I have taught them the things not learned in formal education such as conflict resolution with bill collectors, how algebra really does help with a (income) − b (mortgage) = bankruptcy?

- Not having all the right answers, not being able to help at the right time. Kids change a lot throughout the years, and part of our success as parents is when they are able to make decisions on their own (even at an early age) and stick with those decisions.

- Still, the fear of not being able to help at a crucial moment is what worries me, because I know I can attend to little details on an everyday basis.

- Doing or saying something that will be harmful to my child's emotional and psychological well-being

- Passing on my bad habits and mistakes to my children

- Getting it all wrong

- Making a mistake. Either not doing enough for my children or doing too much. Also hurting their self-esteem by being too honest.

- Not finding the balance between being a helicopter parent and lax parenting

- Knowing that fine line between being a helicopter parent and being an involved parent

- I'm afraid that I'm not properly teaching my child to be confident, dependent, and to have good self-esteem.

- Not making the right choices for my child, or making a decision that could be bad for them

- Doing or saying something that will hurt my child, and it will stay with her for a long time

- Failure

- That I have not taught them how to be a productive citizen

- Not being able to provide for my children, either emotionally or financially

- I always feared that I would not be a good parent—at least by my own standards. My own parents were very good, but like many families, we were not perfect. I was always fearful of continuing the cycle of bad habits and pains that I experienced growing up.

- I'm afraid I'll damage my kids as they become independent adults. I'm afraid that what I say or do now, while they're four to six years old, will someday prevent them from making rational, ethical, moral choices when they're old. I'm afraid that what I do/ say now will somehow prevent them from following their dreams and being happy, successful adults.

- Inadvertently damaging their little psyche or self-esteem

- Trying to be perfect in every area, and wanting the child to understand and appreciate your efforts

- Making mistakes that will come back to haunt my children in the future

- As the child gets older, starting with their teens, not being successful in teaching them how to manage their life demands such as school, athletics, recreational, etc. without succumbing to the high level of pressure. Schoolwork is so demanding, what with going to school all day and then having three to four hours of homework leaves the child with so little time to themselves.

- I am afraid of investing so much energy in their success that I find myself emotionally drained, and they continue to do "their" thing.

- That I will somehow let my son down or disappoint him because we have been thru so much together between two divorces, being rejected by his biological and adoptive father, and then my battle with breast cancer which has caused my son to have to grow up so much more faster than his classmates

- I guess I am afraid they will fail in their futures and it will somehow be my fault. I know better, yet that is a real fear of mine. I do not want them to end up in a lifelong struggle of just making it. I have seen too much of the "just making it" lifestyle, and I want so much more for them.

- I am afraid that my hang-ups or shortcomings will affect my child's well-being and relationships in the long term.

- Failure of instilling good moral values. Not being able to always be there for my children when they need me to be due to outside influences such as work. Work hours can interfere with my being able to experience life-changing events that my children are involved in.

- I am most afraid that I have failed as a parent.

- Not doing enough to help them reach their full potential

- "Dropping the ball" in any way will affect their lives

- Failing to help my kids reach their full potential

- I am afraid of being a single mom and alone. I worry about having the strength to adhere to my convictions and be firm, yet still earning my daughter's respect and love.

- I think my biggest fear is letting go enough for him to experience his own failures and heartbreaks. I wish I could protect him from everything; however, I know that he will never be able to live life if I do.

- Will I be able to provide everything necessary for my children?

- Not being able to adequately provide for my son

- Missing signs that something is wrong. I have a very open relationship with my daughter (thankfully), but when I hear some of the things she tells me about other kids, my first question is "How do her/his parents not know that?" I hope I remain close enough to her to keep that trust and remain in tune with her as she grows up.

- I want my children to be confident without being arrogant, compassionate without being gullible.

- Limiting control...and giving my children the opportunity and freedom to make their own decisions. Realizing that confidence is fostered through guided independence and that mistakes are learning experiences.

- Not being able to provide my children what they will need to be successful, productive adults

- Providing at a level so the child does not have to miss out on different life experiences

- Not being able to provide my kids with the tools they need to be successful since I'm a single parent

- Messing up. Teaching them something or neglecting to teach them something that they will need later in life. Missing out. Being absent during one of life's big moments.

- Shortchanging my children. I don't want to limit them or their exposure to culture, arts, life, or education.

- Providing them with enough love, self-reliance, and education so that they can be happy and successful throughout all phases of their lives

- I am most afraid that I have not given my child the adequate tools (morals, values, drive, and determination) to succeed in his adult life.

- Making the wrong decisions.

- I am afraid that I will be unable to provide sufficient educational support to my child when the teachers are too busy—or to teach them sufficiently how to manage their stress.

- I'm afraid of a lot of things about parenting. It is a "learn as you go" with children. My biggest fear is that my children will be mad with me when I have to punish them, but I do so anyway because I know that is what is best for them and they will thank me later.

After reading through this list of parent responses, take some time to look back over your personal list. Then think about which parent responses resonated with you. Add them to your list, remembering that this group of responses focused on what you are most afraid of as personal failures of when it comes to parenting.

1b. What are you most afraid of when it comes to parenting? 15 percent said Future Success/Happiness of Child.

- Creating lasting resentment toward myself from my child

- I may be unique as a parent as my children are spread out in age. My biggest fears have always involved their physical, mental, and spiritual development. I am most afraid of my children not finding a "perfect" mate to go through life with. I know I will finally be able to relax when all four are happily married.

- I feel I am most afraid of my children not being successful adults, success being defined as independent, self-supporting, and content

- Failure. You see other families with kids doing drugs or getting arrested. You want your children to grow up to be responsible, productive adults.

- I worry most about not effectively equipping my children to face the real world.

- I worry about raising a child that is not a happy, well-adjusted member of society.

- I worry about being able to give my children the knowledge to succeed and how to make critical decisions for themselves. Wanting them to be able to stand on their own.

- Not being able to give my children the opportunities and exposure to find what they love to do and are good at

- I worry that my kids will make bad choices that could affect the rest of their lives. Sometimes kids don't understand the true "consequences" of certain actions they take.

- I most worry about having my kid turn out to be a jailbird or drug addict or some other nonproductive member of society.

- I'm worried about the future. My husband and I try so hard to teach our girls the "right" way to be and the "right" way to do things.

- Lousy education system

- That the child will grow up to be unhappy

- My child not having enough information

- Ensuring my kids grow up to be well-rounded children

- I worry that my children will not come to me when they have an issue or challenge they cannot handle themselves.

- Having my child grow up to be a self-centered, entitled, lazy adult

- I worry that my child will still make detrimental choices while growing up even though we, as parents, communicate expectations and values often and try to instill a nurturing environment.

- Having a child become deceptive, hiding information about a situation, rather than seeking my help

- I worry about how they are going to turn out when they become adults.

After reading through this list of parent responses, take some time to look back over your personal list. Then think about which parent responses resonated with you. Add them to your list, remembering that this group of responses focused on what you are most afraid of regarding your child's future success and happiness.

    1c. What are you most afraid of when it comes to parenting? 13 percent said Safety and Security of Child.

- When my daughter was young, I was most concerned about her safety.

- Safety of my child

- The world and all the crime in it today

- Giving freedom but keeping my child safe as well. I am fearful of automobile accidents with young people.

- The things that you can't see and can only really know if your child tells you (bullying, depression, etc.)

- My child's death

- My child driving recklessly

- The potential for a bullying situation

- That my child will encounter a person with ill intentions

- That my kids are not safe

- Making sure everything is okay with my child

- That something will happen to my child that I have no control over

- That my child may die a premature death

- Any serious health issue that can take my kid's life

- I am most afraid of something bad happening to my children.

- I am most afraid of how others treat my children when I am unable to address things like bullying, driving safety, and peer-related issues.

- Protecting my child from harm

After reading through this list of parent responses, take some time to look back over your personal list. Then think about which parent responses resonated with you. Add them to your list, remembering that this group of responses focused on what you are most afraid of regarding your child's safety and security.

1d. What are you most afraid of when it comes to parenting? 8 percent said Negative Outside Influences on Child.

- I am most afraid of my child going down the wrong path with the wrong friends. Bad influences.

- The negative influences of other people that my kids are exposed to on a daily basis

- I fear the negative influence of others that could potentially alter my children's decision making.

- Having someone with an outside influence, influence my children (either peer pressure or deceit to take advantage of them) in a manner that is self-destructive to my children (drugs, crime)

- My child dealing with peer pressure from other kids, and my child getting the wrong ideas and bad influences at school

- How the world is destroying the core family values and how this is influencing society

- Outside negative influences my children face every day at school and in the media

- The world's views on morality and how sex is portrayed to my children

- The bad influences of the world

- The teen years—influence of friends, hormones, society.

- My son and his adolescent years, as I will face new challenges such as peer pressure, girls, driving, smoking, and the lies that adolescents tend to engage in

After reading through this list of parent responses, take some time to look back over your personal list. Then think about which parent responses resonated with you. Add them to your list, remembering that this group of responses focused on what you are most afraid of regarding outside negative influences on your child.

2a. What do you worry the most about as a parent? 26 percent said Personal Failures as a Parent.

- Screwing my kids up! Patience with them, and the kids becoming successful.

- Not allowing them to learn the consequence from their own mistakes

- Not having taught my children values, manners, character

- Being able to give my child a happy and healthy life

- I worry whether or not I am doing everything possible to help my child be a better person and successful in life.

- I worry most about making mistakes, that something I do will affect my kids' long-term growth.

- Meeting the needs of my child. I have three kids and all three have had different needs. Only have one left at home. Sometimes it feels like I don't have enough time to stay on top of what he needs and to keep him accountable.

- I guess I worry most about whether I am covering all of the important things, whether they be spiritual needs, nutrition, social skills, any number of the important aspects of life. I don't want to lack in any area!

- I worry about getting it "wrong," or missing the things that are important to my children.

- I worry about being financially supportive.

- That I will not be successful in teaching my children to make good decisions in all aspects of their lives

- Have I given my son all the tools he will need to be able to survive in our society?

- I worry that I am giving them a perceived notion that life is easy. Maybe I am doing too much for them. Maybe I am not letting them learn from their mistakes enough. Maybe I am not being a good role model— someone that they can look up to.

- I worry that a stupid mistake brought on by peer pressure will change their lives forever.

- I worry that my daughter will fail because I didn't give the best guidance I could. The question is always, do I need to be more strict? Do I need to be more lenient? I sometimes struggle to find a middle ground. Somewhere in between totally not caring and having my head spin like a crazy person would be great!

- Money

- I worry about giving my child a well-balanced life and exposing them too diverse people, places, and things.

- Being able to be there for my child because I work, and making sure my child is around good influences and has good self-esteem

- Have I prepared my child for adulthood?

- I always try to give my children more than I had as a child. I worry that I may fail at times.

- Am I spending enough time with my kids, and am I focused on them enough?

- I worry about dying before they're independent.

- Am I doing enough/parenting correctly?

- I worry about being confident that I did my job to ensure my children have the ability to make sound decisions.

- Not being able to provide my kids with the tools they need to be successful since I'm a single parent

- My children are all eleven and younger presently. So I worry about whether I am giving them each enough time.

- I worry about meeting all their needs.

- How to effectively show my kids how to be true to themselves but operate within general social structure appropriately. We get a little too caught up in what others think sometimes and need to learn to parent as we see fit.

- I worry about making mistakes that affect my children for the rest of their lives.

- Knowing when to back off and let my child succeed or fail on her own merits

- Finding the middle ground between parenting approaches (not too much of a dictatorship, not too much freedom)

- I worry about whether I have prepared my child to lead an independent life.

- Not being able to provide for my kids to take care if their needs

- The thing that I worry most about my children as a parent is having the resources/finances to allow them to achieve and be the best they can be.

After reading through this list of parent responses, take some time to look back over your personal list. Then think about which parent responses resonated with you. Add them to your list, remembering that this group of responses focused on what you are worried the most about as personal failures when it comes to parenting.

2b. What do you worry the most about as a parent? 25 percent said Future Success/Happiness of Child.

- That they will grow up to happy, hardworking, and good citizens of the world

- I worry that they will choose the wrong path. That they might settle for what life offers instead of following their talents and gifts, which I believe leads to a happy career and fulfilling life.

- That my children will have the right tools to be successful on their own—education, common sense, ability to problem solve, compassion

- I worry most about how poor choices may affect my children, and how they will handle adversity when faced with it.

- That my kids will grow up and not be able to see all of the opportunities available because of learned limited thinking

- That my kids will go through their life hating their job, feeling flat and unsatisfied. I worry that they will grow up with an empty hole that gets filled with ineffective things, such as substances, overeating, conflict, or poor relationships. I want them to have a hunger for life, a passion for learning, a complete full heart, compassion for themselves and others, and lots of laughter and fun along the way.

- I worry about the future.

- I worry about their future. From what they will be when they grow up, will they be able to support themselves, to who is driving them home and is that person a good driver, to who will they marry and will that person have the same beliefs that we have.

- Every day I ask God to care for them and protect them, but some days I take back the worries instead of leaving them in His lap. I worried a lot about their salvation, but at eighteen and twenty that is now secure. I worry about the dumbest things, but they are my babies and I can't help it.

- My children not being happy with themselves

- I worry about my kid turning out to be a jailbird or drug addict or some other nonproductive member of society.

- I worry about my children being content and happy for the most part.

- That the future will be drastically different from the present and my children will not be properly prepared for it

- I worry about guiding my children to become productive, happy adults.

- I worry that the educational system has become so politicalized with standardized testing that it has lost focus on the well-being of children. Kids are not allowed to be kids any longer, and schools have become a negative environment full of stress. We place pressure on children that was meant for adults and then scratch our heads and wonder why they aren't happy.

- I worry most about raising good, wholesome, balanced girls that will grow to be productive members of society.

- My children not learning to be the most self-secure and independent that they can be

- My child not succeeding in their chosen endeavors

- I worry and wonder whether or not my children are far enough along in their walk with God to be sensitive to His direction.

- I worry about creating a well-rounded child who will be a leader, make good choices, and approach me whenever she has a challenge that she cannot face alone. Children hear, see, and do more with all of the peer pressure than what was around when I was young. I want to instill in my children confidence and self-control to make decisions they are satisfied with.

- Their future

- I worry whether my kid will be fine, at his best, when he is not with me.

- I worry about how my child is going to turn out as a person.

- That my kids will not attain their dreams

- The happiness and well-being of my children

- I worry about whether my daughter will be educated and make good life decisions that will make her happy and successful.

- That my kids are respectful, loyal, and honest, and that they absorb most of what their father and I try to teach them

- I worry about proper preparation for the future and for safety at all times.

- My biggest worry is about how my children are treated in the care of others, especially at school.

- That my child will make the same mistakes I did as a youth regarding human intimacy

- I worry about my kids listening and implementing in real-world situations.

- I worry the most that my children are not saved in Christ and that they will take the wrong path in life.

- That my child will feel inadequate

After reading through this list of parent responses, take some time to look back over your personal list. Then think about which parent responses resonated with you. Add them to your list, remembering that this group of responses focused on what you are worried the most about regarding your child's future success and happiness.

2c. What do you worry the most about as a parent? 31 percent said Safety and Security of Child.

- Keeping my child safe from worldly troubles

- Their safety

- My children's well-being—mental, physical, and emotional

- The safety of my children

- The safety of our children as they grow older each year

- My child's safety and picking up bad habits (smoking, drinking, drugs)

- Their health and safety is my biggest concern. It is hard letting go as they become older. You still worry about them and want them to stay well and safe.

- I worry most about my child's safety. I want my children to be protected from bullies and other random acts of violence.

- I worry most about my kid's physical safety.

- The safety of my children—driving, peer pressure, strangers

- The safety of my child and my child's future

- I worry about my kids' safety.

- I am most afraid of my children getting hurt. Today's world is not always a kind place, and there are so many opportunities that are out of my control as soon as they walk out of the house each morning. From peers, to predators, to pressure—it is a lot for a kid to deal with and a heavy weight on the shoulders of parents.

- I worry about the complete health of my children.

- I worry about something tragic happening to my child.

- My child's safety

- My kids getting hurt in an accident, or getting some bad disease

- That something will happen to my child such as an accident. As much as I try to prepare her to be a good driver, accidents always happen. Losing her would be devastating.

- I worry about his health and safety.

- That when my child is away from my care that he is safe and being looked after by the adult in charge

- My children's all-around safety

- My kids getting hurt in an accident

- The safety of my teen when she is out at social events. While I believe she will make good decisions (most of the time), I am concerned about the behavior of other teens who may be violent, have weapons, driving recklessly or "under the influence," and how she might be affected.

- I worry about their safety.

- Death. So afraid of losing one of my children.

- My children's ability to "fend for themselves" in the wilds of society

- Ensuring my child's safety when she is not with me

- I worry about a lot! Mostly, I worry about her health.

- Safety

- My child getting hurt or being harmed…not living up to their possibilities. Will they be a good person?

- I am worried about my child's safety.

- I worry about dying before both my children are adults.

- Their overall safety

- That something will happen to my child that I could have prevented

- The safety of my child

- The health and safety of my children is paramount. As the kids get older and they have more freedom, I always worry about them driving or dangers with Internet use.

- I worry that something awful will happen to my kids.

- Something horrible happening to them or to me (leaving them without a parent)

- My children's safety

After reading through this list of parent responses, take some time to look back over your personal list. Then think about which parent responses resonated with you. Add them to your list, remembering that this group of responses focused on what you are worried the most about regarding your child's safety and security.

2d. What do you worry the most about as a parent? 18 percent said Negative Outside Influences on Child.

- That outside influences, if not monitored properly, could wind up changing the way I would want my children to perceive how the world really is and the way I would want them to present themselves to the world

- I worry about what the world will do to my daughters once they leave my home and my constant supervision.

- I worry about my children not being strong enough to stand up to the persecution for their faith in God and being bullied.

- I worry about her stress and her ability to be outspoken and stand for what she believes is right.

- I worry most that my son will get in with the wrong crowd because of peer pressure, regardless of everything we have taught him.

- I am most worried about my children getting mixed up with the wrong people and not being saved in the eyes of the Lord.

- Even though my sons are on the right track, I worry about them being derailed by a single or series of bad decisions.

- Alcohol and substance abuse. Extremely heavy family history in those areas.

- I worry about negative influences, what they are absorbing from the world around them (values, self-esteem, etc.).

- My children getting mixed up with the wrong crowd

- I worry about the world we live in and how hard it's going to be when they are my age.

- I worry that the kids will be influenced by peer pressure and do things that may get them into a bad situation.

- Other children's influence

- At this point, I worry about my older son (six years old) learning or experiencing things I am not ready for him to know about (i.e., sexuality, violence, sadness, death).

- It changes daily. Today I am concerned about how little face-to-face time children have with one another outside of school. Unless they are in school or in a club, they are socializing through media. Not good.

- I worry about outside influences and temptation.

- I worry most that my child will be influenced, by other children, to do drugs or other bad behavior.

- My children being bullied and not being able to give my children everything they need

- I worry about others teasing my daughter and her not knowing what to say.

- Outside negative influences affecting my child's decision making. Pressure on kids to be "good" at everything and every subject.

- My son growing up with bullies and an uncertain future as it relates to education, retirement, etc.

- I worry about my kids getting into trouble due to improper behavior.

After reading through this list of parent responses, take some time to look back over your personal list. Then think about which parent responses resonated with you. Add them to your list, remembering that this group of responses focused on what you are worried the most about regarding outside negative influences on your child.

## Closed-Ended Responses for Survey Questions 3–5

The last three survey questions were closed-ended and allowed parents to choose from a set of answer choices. For questions 3 and 4, the answer choices followed a scale or continuum from Routinely to Never. The answer choices for question 5 were based on a continuum denoting frequency from Weekly to Never.

3. How often are you getting the results with your child that you thought you would get?

    a. 35 percent Routinely

    b. 60 percent Often

    c. 4 percent Rarely

    d. 1 percent Never

Keeping in mind that the same parents responded to all five questions, it's interesting to note that a majority of the parents, 60 percent of them, responded that, with their child, they Often get the results that they thought they would get. If you combine that response with those that answered Routinely, that's an impressive 95 percent of parents. It would appear from these percentages that, in general, the parents believed that they were being successful in achieving the results they expected with their children. When you compare the favorable response for question 3 to the responses for questions 1 and 2, it is a bit surprising, given the large number of fear and worry statements.

After discussing this inconsistency with parents, I've concluded that it appears their conscious mind tended to report favorably on their level of success in parenting, but when asked about their parenting fears and worries, their subconscious mind, where the limiting beliefs hang out, served up an ample supply of concerns when it came to raising their kids.

Another example of this phenomenon of an apparent inconsistency in survey responses is found in a 2013 publication by the National Opinion Research Center (NORC) at the University of Chicago. A report was issued titled "Parents' Attitudes on the Quality of Education in the United States." This survey research report sought to gain the perspectives and opinions of parents of their students between kindergarten and twelfth grade during the 2012–13 school year. As is typical in public opinion surveys, parents rated the quality of education in public schools across the United States significantly less positively, with 38 percent terming it good or excellent, than the quality of education their own child received in local public schools, with 57 percent terming it good or excellent.

In other words, parent respondents in the education survey tended to evaluate their own personal experience more favorably than when answering survey questions about education in general. I see this as being similar to parents generally tending to rate themselves as having higher levels of satisfaction with the results they are getting with their children, but providing a less satisfying picture when asked questions about fears and worries. It's all about our beliefs and perceptions as parents and how willing we are to be completely honest with ourselves.

4. How often do you experience "epic fails" in parenting and just don't understand why?

   a. <1 percent Routinely

   b. 19 percent Frequently

   c. 74 percent Rarely

   d. 6 percent Never

Taking a look at the survey responses for question 4, parents indicated by a large majority, 80 percent, that, in parenting, they either Rarely or Never experienced large failures with little to no understanding behind the cause of the failure. Once again, even though parents are reporting that they aren't experiencing large failures, it is quite clear when you review their responses for questions 1 and 2 that their subconscious is conjuring up all sorts of fears and worries about potential failures that span across all four categories discussed earlier.

In chapter 2 we talked about great parenting being intentional. We have to start by intentionally confronting our beliefs and making assessments about which ones are actually limiting us. It is only when we can be honest about what is coming from our subconscious mind that we can begin to acknowledge our limiting beliefs and take steps toward changing those thought patterns. We will discuss more about how to do this in chapters 5 and 6.

5. How often do you read parenting books, magazines, or blogs?

   a. 10 percent Weekly

   b. 19 percent Monthly

   c. 23 percent Every Few Months

   d. 36 percent Rarely

   e. 12 percent Never

Survey question number 5 was asked to get a feel for how often parents were accessing and utilizing parenting resources and if it appeared to have any relationship to their perceived levels of success.

A total of 48 percent of parents who responded fell into the Rarely or Never categories for reading parenting books, magazines, or blogs. Another 23 percent indicated that they only accessed these resources every few months, which probably did not make a significant impact on their parenting knowledge, attitudes, beliefs, or behaviors. This survey question result could indicate that even though parents expressed some significant fears and worries about their own potential parenting failures and insecurities and their child's future success and happiness, they clearly were not, in general, seeking out parenting resources to assist them in achieving more successful outcomes or planning for future challenges. Again, apparently living life/parenting on autopilot.

Once again, I believe that the results of this survey question indicate that parents go day after day, year after year, with significant fears, worries, and insecurities about raising kids that succeed, yet they do not understand the impact of their own limiting belief system on parenting outcomes.

The good news is that by intentionally increasing our awareness of our limiting beliefs and how they impact our parenting, we can begin to break this cycle in the parenting of our children. Then and only then can we as parents begin to see the enormous power in being intentional about challenging our limiting beliefs and replacing them with empowering beliefs. This is the beginning of a revolutionary approach to *Raising Kids That Succeed!*

In the next chapter, I'll share with you some more specific things you can do as a parent to begin to break this cycle of limiting beliefs. You should be feeling excited right now, having learned what you have learned to this point and knowing the incredibly important part you play as a parent when you choose to become empowered to literally change the course and destiny of an entire generation!

# CHAPTER 5

## BREAKING THE CYCLE OF LIMITING BELIEFS

As the title of this chapter implies, it's not enough for us as parents to find and change our own limiting beliefs. We must also focus on breaking the cycle of transferring them to our kids, if they are to overcome life's limitations and think their way to lifelong successes. You see, it's not really life's external limitations that are the problem for our kids. It's our kids' perceptions/beliefs of life's external limitations and their own internal limiting beliefs that cause the real problems. Before we can start them on their own journey of self-awareness and being able to challenge their own limiting beliefs, we will have set them on a course for a change in their thinking habits that will serve them well for the rest of their lives! That means a change from limiting beliefs (LB) to empowering beliefs (EB). Now that's something to get excited about!

Remember…Fears + Worries = Limiting Beliefs Clues

In the last chapter, you had a great opportunity to create your own list of fears and worries as a parent, as well as read the fears and worries of other parents. You probably were able to add to your list as you reviewed the survey responses and saw statements that resonated with you.

I also mentioned in a previous chapter that we would take a look at how those fear and worry statements were actually providing clues to underlying limiting beliefs that need to be challenged and then changed to empowering beliefs.

Let's take a look at some of the parent survey responses...

A whopping 64 percent of the parent responses about fears fell into the Personal Failure as a Parent category. This is a strong indication of an existence of very limiting feelings and beliefs of the parent. Here are some examples:

- Being a bad influence on my kids through my own weaknesses

- Not being the best example

- Hoping that my mistakes in parenting will not scar my children

- That I will disappoint my child or that he will feel unloved

- That I am somehow going to "screw something up" and my kids won't reach their potential for success

- That I'm not giving my child the best childhood ever

- Failing in my marriage and becoming a single parent

- Getting it all wrong

Using what you now know and understand about what limiting beliefs sound like, can you see the underlying limitations in these fear statements? Go back to your notes or journal and change each of these fear statements into a limiting belief statement. Start each one with "I am" or "I will" or "My…"

For example, the first one listed,

Being a bad influence on my kids through my own weaknesses

becomes…

I am a bad influence on my kids through my own weaknesses.

If you really want to go more in-depth and explore this method of restating fear and worry statements as LB statements, you can actually do this exercise with each of the survey responses in all four of the categories listed in chapter 4. It's a real eye-opener!

I think after completing this activity, it will be pretty clear to you that, if we are to be successful in breaking this cycle with our kids, we all have a large number of limiting beliefs lurking in our subconscious that need to be transitioned into empowering beliefs. And I believe it's important that we first think more about exactly what empowering beliefs are and how to successfully incorporate them into our thinking habits.

Author Mikael Olsson, in his book *Handbook of Success: How to Make Your Life What You Want It to Be*, explains some important things about the concept of empowering beliefs. He shares that there are many empowering beliefs that can enhance your quality of life. You can find them by considering what you would have to believe in order to be, have, or do what you want in life.

Olsson also shares a list of empowering beliefs that contains some useful generalizations or assumptions. They may not always be "true" for you yet, but by convincing yourself that they are and acting as if you believe them, you will begin to see the world from a more resourceful perspective. According to Olsson:

- There is no failure, only feedback. What we learn from every experience and every response is only information that tells you whether you are being effective or not.

- There are no problems, only challenges. Every obstacle is actually a stepping stone toward success to help you learn and grow.

- There is no fear, only excitement. Let your fears motivate you to overcome them instead of hold you back.

- If what I am doing is not working, I will try something else. Be flexible and do not resist change. For something new to happen, you have to try something different.

- No matter what happens, I can handle it. Become confident that you can deal with anything that may happen in your life.

- My past does not equal my future. At any point in time, you can change any part of your life.

- I am destined for success. Become absolutely convinced that you are a success in the making (and that your kids are, too!).

- Everyone is secretly helping me to succeed. The concept of pronoia (the opposite of paranoia)— assume the best of intentions of everyone around you.

- Anyone can do anything, and anything is possible. If one person in the world can do it, anybody can by figuring out how they are doing it.

- I am free to choose my own destiny. Accept that you are in control of your own life, decisions, and actions.

Take the time now to go back and look at the list of fear and worry statements that you converted to LB statements. Decide which of Olsson's EB statements would apply to each LB statement. For example...

Being a bad influence on my kids through my own weaknesses

becomes...

I am a bad influence on my kids through my own weaknesses. (LB)

becomes...

There is no failure, only feedback. What we learn from every experience and every response is only information that tells us whether we are being effective or not. (EB)

So for parents, here are the steps to breaking the cycle of limiting beliefs:

- Discover Parent Limiting Beliefs

- Change Parent Limiting Beliefs to Empowering Beliefs

- Discover Child Limiting Beliefs

- Change Child Limiting Beliefs to Empowering Beliefs

- Child Empowering Beliefs lead to Thinking Their Way to Lifelong Successes

So far, we've talked about your limiting beliefs and empowering beliefs. Now let's spend some time talking about how to discover your child's limiting beliefs and some ways to change them to empowering beliefs.

## Discovering Your Child's Limiting Beliefs

How do parents gain an awareness of their children's limiting beliefs? That's an extremely important question. We've already discussed some ways that you can begin to probe your own subconscious and shine a bright light on your own limiting beliefs. To a great degree, the process is much the same for discovering your children's limiting beliefs. Obviously, you become the guide and facilitator and take the initiative in this process.

There is a variety of ways that parents can gain an awareness of their children's limiting beliefs. Listening to what your children say about themselves is one of the very best ways to begin gaining an awareness of the limiting beliefs that have already begun in your children's thinking. Begin to pay close attention each time your children make statements that limit themselves in having success in any kind of situation. For example, have you ever heard your child say, "I'm not good at math" or how about, "I'm not good at sports"? Or have you heard them say, "No one wants to be my friend," or even, "Everyone is picking on me?"

As the phases of development and growth occur in children, parents will begin to see different kinds of limiting belief statements coming from them. In the early years, we don't hear our children saying very many limiting things about themselves. For example, when our toddlers are learning to walk, and we see them try again and again to pull themselves up to stand for a few seconds and then fall. Even if they're not able to speak yet, you don't see negative facial expressions or see them stop trying. Instead, they have a belief system that tells them, "I didn't make it that time, but I'm going to try again!" And they do. They try again and again until they are finally successful. After that, the rest is history.

Or how about something as simple as learning to ride a bike? Few kids stop trying to learn to ride just because they don't immediately succeed. Through trial and error, they learn about their ability to hold their balance, as well as things that seem counterintuitive, like the faster you pedal, the easier it is to ride. There aren't many kids who never learn to ride a bike. On their own, they don't have a limiting belief that tells them they can't do it.

There are other examples you will see as you go through watching your children grow and develop. As you become more observant, it will become obvious to you that the longer children are out in the world interacting at school with friends or in organized play or athletics, the more their limiting beliefs begin to grow. Listen to what they say about themselves. Listen to what they say about others.

A great exercise for a parent is to begin listening for and writing down the limiting beliefs you hear your child speak. Even if you're not big on journaling, just take down some private notes for yourself in your smart phone or whatever way works for you. Chances are, you will be amazed at the list you compile over a short period of time.

Only you can determine when you want to begin your conversation with your child about the LB statements that you've recorded. The younger the child, the more important it is to catch the statements as they actually occur, so you can help your child change the LB into an EB. For example, if your child says, "No one in my class likes me," you can take this as a teachable moment and say, "I know it might seem to you that no one in your class likes you, but I'll bet you can think of some friends in your class that have done things that show they do like you. Tell me about those friends and what they did." From there, you can lead your child to restate the original LB statement into something more realistic and empowering like, "Although I am not close friends with every person in my class, I have many friends in my class who like me."

It is extremely important to identify and change your child's LB statements to EB statements when they occur. When you begin to record the LB statements, be sure to gauge the prevalence of your child's LB statements and whether or not you see any pattern to them.

As you become more aware while listening to and processing your child's statements, keep in mind that your own limiting beliefs can actually hinder your ability to recognize them in your kids. This is because we tend to overlook the limiting belief statements we are still holding on to. Remember that it's critical for us to take this journey for ourselves and increase our awareness of our own limiting beliefs so we can more easily recognize them in our kids.

My favorite book says that we should "first cast out the beam out of your own eye; and then shall you see clearly to cast out the mote out of your brother's eye" (Matthew 7:5 AKJV). We can't even hope to recognize stifling, sabotaging, and paralyzing limiting beliefs in our kids if we haven't dealt with the same ones in our own lives.

In a very real way, this whole new way of thinking and interacting is becoming an awakened parent. In an excerpt from the book *Becoming an Awakened Parent*, authors Denny Hagel and Benni Heacock share the following thoughts:

> First, becoming an Awakened Parent means to be clear about what you desire from your parenting experience and what benefits you want your children to receive as a result of your role in their lives. Do you want your children to be independent thinkers with confidence and a healthy self-esteem or do you want them to conform to the thoughts, ideas, and beliefs of others?

> The second is to understand how to raise your children to approach life from a place of strength, confidence, and inner peace, empowered with an understanding of the law of attraction at work in their lives. You will thus be providing them with the confidence and skills to experience life in a way that supports who they truly are. The key to a successful parenting journey for you and your children is to become the best parent you can be in order to raise empowered children.

> It is always easier to accept a new concept when there are no pre-conceived ideas to get in the way. And believe it or not, regardless of your lifestyle or level of self-growth, by virtue of the simple fact that you have gone through your own childhood, you do have some pre-conceived ideas about parenting. These ideas are automatically formed by the way your parents chose to parent you. Even if at this point in your life you disagree with the manner in which you were parented, some of those ideas are deeply embedded in your subconscious mind and affect your choices without your awareness. Have you ever found yourself speaking

to your children and the words that came out of your mouth were the exact words that once came from your mother's mouth? And those were the words you vowed when you were a child you would NEVER speak to your children? Regardless of your background or how you were parented, there are probably very few who haven't had that "Oh No…" experience. Here's the solution. The "missing secret to parenting" is not based on a professional's opinion or an expert's theory; it is based on your parenting mindset, passed down or of conscious choice.

Hagel and Heacock go on to say that being "aware" is key to being an awakened parent. The specific aspects to consider are to become:

- Aware of your role in your child's life

- Aware of your child's individuality

- Aware of your child's personality

- Aware of your child's learning style

- Aware of your impact on your child

- Aware of your child's reaction to your parenting style

- Aware of your interaction/communication with your child

- Aware of the goals you have for your child

- Aware of the goals your child has for himself/herself

- Aware of the effectiveness of your impact on these goals (both yours and your child's)

As you can see from this list, there are many "awarenesses" to pay attention to as an awakened parent. They are all equally important in creating a successful outcome. And, in the end, the outcome you desire to achieve is empowered children who know how to recognize their own limiting beliefs and who possesses the tools to change them to empowering beliefs so they can begin to think their way to lifelong successes!

In the final chapter of this book, I will share the five keys to *Raising Kids That Succeed*, based upon the previous insights of this book. Keep your notes or journal handy as we discuss these important keys and how to put into action what you've learned.

# CHAPTER 6

## THE FIVE KEYS TO RAISING KIDS THAT SUCCEED

When we think about the "keys" to something, we tend to automatically think about doors. If a door is locked, then we need a key of some sort to unlock it. I decided to use the concept of "keys" in providing a summary and action plan for parents because the more I thought about this whole process, the more it conjured up a picture of doors in our thinking processes. These doors are either blocking our desired destination or being opened to allow us to walk through to new and more successful destinations. The success that we all desire in our own lives and in the lives of our children lies within our reach if we just take the time to learn and apply these five important keys to *Raising Kids That Succeed.*

You may recall that the subtitle of this book is *How to Help Your Kids Overcome Life's Limitations and Think Their Way to Lifelong Successes.* This final chapter is going to help you organize and synthesize the major points we've discussed so far in this book so you will have an action plan at your fingertips as you begin to implement these life-changing thinking keys.

## The Five Keys

In my many years as a school administrator, I always had a large set of keys to carry around. Often, the school campus had several different buildings and each building had its own set of keys. With all of those keys jingling around, it was a pretty daunting task to remember which keys went to which building. I came up with color-code systems, used different kinds of key chains, and created any other method I could think of to cut down on my confusion and the time it took to find the key I needed.

If you've ever had a similar experience, then you can appreciate the concept of the "master key." The master key is your best friend. It's the key that will work in most all doors when you can't seem to quickly find the individual door key you need. Master keys are highly protected because, obviously, this one key will open many doors. It's perhaps the most important key you carry around with you every day. So with that thought in mind, I'm calling Key #1 the Master Key.

## Key #1 – The Master Key

Continuing to use and building upon my key ring example, the Master Key is the overarching and supporting mind-set that a parent must first have before attempting to engage in discovering and identifying their own limiting beliefs and transforming them into empowering beliefs. Here is the Master Key:

No matter where you are in your parenting journey,

it's never too late to Change, Improve, Learn,

Confront *limiting beliefs* and replace them with

*empowering beliefs.*

That means that any place you fall on the parenting spectrum, from not yet being a parent, to being a parent with adult children, it really doesn't matter. It's never too early or too late to engage in the self-discovery required for this important journey. I've even helped parents of adult children engage in this process and, in so doing, dramatically improved their relationships with each other. New ways of thinking and believing replaced old, sabotaging belief systems that had long strained their relationships. If you haven't yet added this Master Key to your key ring, then take the time to do it now.

## Key #2 – The Thinking Key

In chapter 1 of this book, I stated that "great parenting requires great thinking." This key simply says that we have to do a good deal of thinking about what we want to create as we engage in parenting. It means that effective parenting is much more about us as parents and who we are and our thinking than it is about who our kids are, at least in the beginning. The Thinking Key gives us the power to take charge of life by thinking, contemplating, reflecting, and knowing our attitudes, beliefs, and insights all along the way. It requires honesty and authenticity, first with ourselves and then with others. The Thinking Key unlocks the doors of exploration and progress and helps us walk away from ignorance and apathy. It's a key that only a small percentage of people routinely use. Choose to use the Thinking Key every day.

## Key #3 – The Intent Key

In chapter 2, I shared that "great parenting is intentional." The Intent Key allows us to be deliberate about what we do. It means that we contemplate our actions and behaviors before we act. It means that we are premeditated in our selection of words, behaviors, attitudes, and beliefs. The Intent Key allows us to unlock the doors of purpose and design. Without being intentional, we can never hope to change our deeply ingrained limiting beliefs. Without being intentional, we can never hope to do the sometimes painful work of transforming our limiting beliefs to empowering beliefs. Using the Intent Key, we can gain access to a world in which we are no longer drifting from day to day on autopilot, filled with fear and worry or engaging in self-blame when we don't achieve the desired parenting outcomes. Make your own personal commitment to grab on to this key and become intentional.

## Key #4 – The Discovery and Empowerment Key

In previous chapters, I discussed in-depth Identifying Limiting Beliefs, The Impact of Limiting Beliefs, and Breaking the Cycle of Limiting Beliefs. A succinct way to communicate the message of those chapters is through the use of the Discovery and Empowerment Key.

Just as a reminder, I shared with you that for parents, there are steps to breaking the cycle of limiting beliefs:

- Discover Parent Limiting Beliefs

- Change Parent Limiting Beliefs to Empowering Beliefs

- Discover Child Limiting Beliefs

- Change Child Limiting Beliefs to Empowering Beliefs

- Child Empowerment Beliefs lead to Thinking Their Way to Lifelong Successes

The Discovery and Empowerment Key reminds us of the two-tiered process: discover our own limiting beliefs and change them to empowering beliefs, and discover our children's limiting beliefs and teach them to change these to empowering beliefs. Making this process an intentional thinking habit will allow us to unlock the doors of personal happiness and lifelong success not only for our children, but also for ourselves.

## Key #5 – The Legacy Key

I would guess that there are many reasons people decide to become a parent. Although I didn't ask that question in my parent survey, a common reason I hear is that people want to continue their family name or, in other words, bring another life into the world. I think what they are trying to communicate in many ways is that they want to leave a legacy. If you looked up the word *legacy* in a dictionary, you would find one of the definitions is, "anything handed down from the past, as from an ancestor or predecessor." There is actually a non-profit group in the United States called the Legacy Parenting Project, which was created with the intent to educate, equip, and encourage moms and dads to parent with purpose. I can't think of a better way to describe the Legacy Key.

Parenting with purpose is really what we've been discussing throughout this book. Author Stephen R. Covey, in his well-known book, *The 7 Habits of Highly Effective People*, says in Habit #2 to "Begin with the End in Mind." This habit is based on imagination, the ability to envision the future, and, in this case, your child's future. Beginning with the end in mind means doing everything you can now to build the legacy that you desire through thinking, intentionality, discovery, and empowerment. The Legacy Key allows us to build a life of purpose and direction for our child instead of a life left to worry, fear, and chance. Understanding the power of the Legacy Key unlocks the door to *Raising Kids That Succeed*, not just now but for generations to come. That is because this legacy is self-perpetuating and will literally transform our world one family at a time.

Grab hold of these five keys with all your might! Don't let limiting beliefs, fear, or worry keep you from experiencing the life you've always imagined you could have. Make the decision today to do the hard work of personal awareness and discovery that will allow you to unlock the same doors for your children and usher them into their own lifetime of true happiness and lifelong success.

Happy Parenting!

# REFERENCES

Dyer, Wayne W. (2001). *What Do You Really Want for Your Children?* New York: Harper Collins.

Dyer, Wayne W. (2014). *I Can See Clearly Now*. New York: Hay House, Inc.

Falconer, Joel. (2013). "Find and Replace Limiting Beliefs, Part 1." Retrieved from http://www.lifehack.org/articles/lifehack/find-replace-limiting-beliefs-part-1-search-techniques.html

Foskett, Allison. (2012). *How Smart Women Achieve Big Goals*. Edmonton: iUniverse.

Foskett, Allison. (2014). "Identifying and Overcoming Limiting Beliefs." Retrieved from http://www.goal-setting-motivation.com/set-your-goals/overcoming-limiting-beliefs/

Hagel, Denny and Benni Heacock. (2010). "Becoming an Awakened Parent." Retrieved from http://missingsecrettoparenting.com/awakened-parenting-free-resources/awakened-parent

Hay, Louise L. (1984). *You Can Heal Your Life*. New York: Hay House.

James, Matthew B. (2013). "4 Steps to Release Limiting Beliefs Learned from Childhood." Retrieved from http://www.psychologytoday.com/blog/focus-forgiveness/201311/4-steps-release-limiting-beliefs-learned-childhood

Johnson, Dani. (2009). *Grooming the Next Generation for Success*. Shippensburg, PA: Destiny Image.

Maxwell, John C. (2009). *How Successful People Think*. New York: Hachette Book Group.

Olsson, Mikael. (2011). "The Year of the Awakened Parent." Retrieved from http://ezinearticles.com/?2010---The-Year-of-the-Awakened-Parent&id=3516117

Osteen, Joel. (2004). *Your Best Life Now: 7 Steps to Living at Your Full Potential*. New York: Hatchett Book Group.

Robbins, T. (2014). "Stop Your Limiting Beliefs: 10 Empowering Beliefs that Will Change Your Life." Retrieved from http://training.tonyrobbins.com/stop-your-limiting-beliefs-10-empowering-beliefs-that-will-change-your-life/

Tompson, Trevor, Jennifer Benz, and Jennifer Agiesta. (2013). Parents' Attitudes Final Report. Retrieved from http://www.joycefdn.org/assets/1/7/Parents_Attitudes_FINAL_Report.pdf

# Dr. Lynn Wicker

Accredited trainer in Behavioral Studies

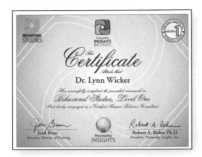

Dr. Lynn Wicker is an accredited trainer in Behavioral Studies in association with Personality Insights, Inc., Atlanta, GA. She is certified to lead seminars and workshops in the DISC Model of Human Behavior as well as administer Adult, Teen and Children DISC Personality assessments. She also offers coaching services for parents and educators as a follow up to the DISC assessments to assist them in gaining a deeper understanding of the assessment reports.

# Resource Materials

## ADULT VERSION

# Discovery
## REPORT
### Online Assessment

**The Discovery Report** is our most comprehensive personality assessment product. This is our standard adult profile version. You will receive a 50-page computer-generated report (sent to you by email) that is highly accurate and easy-to-understand.

The Discovery Report™ is based on the results of an online personality assessment that will take you only about 15-20 minutes to complete.

---

## CHILD VERSION

Online

# Discovery
## REPORT

This one-of-a-kind assessment is designed specifically for children. It is a fun and interactive way for parents and teachers to gain insights into individual preferences or choices the child makes based on robot characters (BOTS).

The stories allow children as young as 5 years old to complete the assessment.

### Ages 5 - 12

*Online Assessment*

## www.lynnwicker.com

# Resource Materials

## Teen Version

Online

**Discovery**
REPORT

**Ages 13 - 22**

*Online Assessment*

**The Get Real! Discovery Report** is our most comprehensive personality assessment product. This is the teen version. You will receive a 58-page computer-generated report (downloaded file) that is highly accurate and easy-to-understand. The Discovery Report is based on the results of an online personality assessment that will take you only about 15-20 minutes to complete online.

## Assessments in Print

### Adult Profile Assessment
• Self-generating graphs for understanding your special personality style blend
• Begin to explore and define your unique style
• DISCover your true personality!

### Get Real!

A personality assessment and development handbook for teenagers. This booklet helps teens learn about their personality styles as well as various vocations for which they would be best suited.

### All About Bots! All About You!

A personality assessment for children. This booklet helps parents and children (ages 5-12) learn about their personality styles. Helpful tips for child rearing are included for parents.

# ABOUT THE AUTHOR

A published author and certified speaker, trainer, and success coach, Dr. Lynn Wicker has thirty years of experience in public education. Holding various leadership positions in K-12 and higher education, including director of a developmental research school, Lynn is an international teacher of transformational leadership principles and uses her "adding value" lifestyle to connect with people creating life transformations. Lynn's passion and purpose in life is to inspire individuals to find their own successes in life and live lives of purpose and meaning. Her education includes a doctorate in education from Florida State University, as well as completing the Harvard Graduate School of Education Superintendent Institute.

**To connect with the Author:**

Lynn Wicker Social Media Links

YouTube:     http://www.youtube.com/c/LynnWicker
LinkedIn:     https://www.linkedin.com/in/lynnwicker
Facebook:     https://www.facebook.com/drlynnwicker/
Twitter:     https://twitter.com/lynn_wicker
Website:     http://www.johncmaxwellgroup.com/lynnwicker/
            http://www.lynnwicker.com/